MAKE NEWS!
MAKE NOISE!

How To Get Publicity For Your Book

by
Shelly Roberts

PARADIGM
Publishing Company

San Diego, California

Other Paradigm Publishing Books by Shelly Roberts:

The Dyke Detector
(How to Tell the Real Lesbians from Ordinary People)

Hey Mom, Guess What!
(150 Ways to Tell Your Mother)

Copyright © 1994 by Shelly Roberts.
All Rights Reserved.

No part of this book may be reproduced or transmitted in any form or by any means electronic or mechanical, except in the case of reviews, without written permission from Paradigm Publishing Company, P.O. Box 3877, San Diego, CA 92163.

Typesetting by Paradigm Publishing Company
Copy Editing by Andrea L.T. Peterson

Printed in the United States of America on acid free paper

Library of Congress Catalog Number: 93-87210
ISBN 1-882587-03-0

Make News! Make Noise!
Table of Contents

Make News! Make Noise! 1
Breaking Through. 4
The Title Tells The Tale. 5
Make News. 6
...Or Make Noise. 8
What To Expect From Your Publisher. 10
Do Not Go Naked Into That Good Fight. 13
There's A Difference Between Ego And Business. 15
Baiting Hooks. 17
All The News That Fits In Print. 19
    Let's Start With The Biggies. 19
    You Can't Make Book On The Book Editor. 20
    Going National. 22
    Making It Into The Mags. 22
    Serving The Special Interests. 22
    What Did You Say? 23
    Do It Yourself. 23
    Print References. 23
Radio Daze. 24
    Breaking Through The Screen. 25
    Out Of Town Is Different. 27
    And Now, Live, In Our Studio... 28
    Radio References. 32
TV Jeebies. 33
    Making The Evening News. 34
    You're The Expert. 35
    Make The Producer's Life Easier. 36
    What You Need To Know On The Air. 37
    TV References. 39
Talk Fast. You Have Fifteen Seconds. 40
    Less Is Better! Write Tight. 41
    Learn From Your Rejections. 42
    ...Heeeeeeeere's You. 42
    You Owe Me One For These. 43
Okay, Okay, Do A Press Release. 44
Hug Your Bookstore. 47
    Stop In And Drop Off. 48
    Sign Here. 50
The Practical Art Of Cross-Ruffing. 52
One-Of-A-Kinds. 54
A Short Thought On A Computer. 55
The Last Word. 56

To Tom, Karen, Robert, Mia, Bobby, and Meg. You know who you are and what you did. What you don't know is how grateful I am to you for it. No, No, thank you.

1
Make News! Make Noise!

Congratulations on getting your book published. It's going to fail.

What! How can I say that?

Easy. It's a matter of fact. I've never read it. I don't have any idea how much time and sweat you put into it. I don't know how good, bad, monumental, or inconsequential your masterpiece is. I only know one thing. If everybody you know personally, including your mother, all your aunts and cousins, and your second grade teacher, buys a copy of your book, your book will fail.

But don't worry. Every book starts out from the contract as a failure.

Well, let me restate that. Nearly every book.

If your name is Clancy, Steele, or Grisham, you can pretty much put your feet up and wait for the limo. The most you have to worry about is how you're going to work all those personal appearances and party invitations into your schedule and still find the time to get another book out. The publicity department of your publisher has already kicked into action. They have you booked on any show that makes a difference, Parade Magazine is already planning an in-depth interview with your grandmother's maid's grown daughter, and the hosts of the Good Morning TV shows are saving you their best smiles. The most work you'll have to do to publicize your latest is to try to remember what city you're in now. As for the rest of us, they rarely send limos to fetch us, especially on the first or second book.

If this is your first book, good going. It was no mean feat to get it into print. And it will be nearly as much work to get somebody you never met before to slide a credit card out of his or her wallet to take it home.

If you've done this before, but just didn't have the reaction you secretly dreamed of all your life, and would like a better chance at having to sign autographs in your old neighborhood, stick around. There may be a trick or two in here you hadn't thought of.

Getting a book noticed is a feat requiring a very large chunk of your attention. Getting it to bestseller is a fluke.

Now let me stop for a moment to let you know who I am, and why, if I'm writing a book on how to publicize your book, you've never heard of me. Well, maybe only some of you have never heard of me. I do have a couple of bestsellers to my name. Not, unfortunately, *New York Times* bestsellers, but bestsellers in their category. I actually have a number of books published, each to a specialty market. And each one was enough of a success *in its category* so that some publisher somewhere asked me to do another one. In 1977 I wrote a humor book to the emerging feminist market. Actually, I wrote *What To Do With A Liberated Woman*, for the suddenly disenfranchised male half of the population. In the early eighties, I wrote *Executive Cool, A Businesswoman's Guide To Surviving Middle Management*. And in the late eighties, I did *I'm Sorry, But I Don't Speak Hexadecimal* to the fledgling computer market. All of these were well received by their intended audiences.

So you see, you don't have to have a blockbuster book jamming the New York front window of Barnes & Noble to be considered a success in the book writing business. You just have to do enough business to get your publisher to ask you to do it again.

In 1992 Paradigm Publishing Company brought out a humor book of mine called, *The Dyke Detector, How To Tell The Real Lesbians From Ordinary People*. The book was also obviously written to a specialty market, and the publisher didn't hold out the hope that she could retire to the Caribbean on the proceeds.

What she didn't reckon on, however, was my twenty plus years as an advertising executive, my tour of duty as a vice president of the largest advertising agency in the world, or my determination. I vowed to take a slim, but, if I do say so myself, hysterically funny, (All through this, we'll talk about what you can and should "say so yourself" about your own book.) volume as far as my training and experience could get it in a fairly short time.

Did it work?

Here are just some of the things that happened. The book sold out its first printing in less than five months to a crossover mainstream market, which is unheard of in this category for a relative unknown. It made the distributor's bestseller list, the list that bookstores order from, publishers pay attention to, and talk show producers peruse for potential guests.

As a result of the kinds of things I did, I got my own radio show. The publisher of the first book went to contract *sight unseen* on the next book, and now has me scheduled to do at least two more in the next two years. Beyond those, I was asked to do *this* book for you.

Here's what it cost: *a lot!*

It cost some actual hard-cash-savings-account-money, some time, and more importantly, a major amount of lost income. I am an independent advertising consultant, which meant I didn't have to answer to a boss who thought nights and weekends were swell times for book promotion, but I virtually gave up my business and my income for a period of time to pursue the necessary publicity. Which meant, of course, that, since I am not independently wealthy, I had to live a lot closer to the edge than I was happy doing for a while. I'm not suggesting that you walk right up to the rim of the bankruptcy cliff on behalf of your own book, only that you make choices that make sense for yourself about how much you're willing to do, and how much you're willing to pay to get your book noticed. It can be costly. How costly depends on just how much time and effort you want to devote to getting your book noticed. How much your book gets noticed depends on how much effort you devote. Frankly, there were moments of total terror in the process.

Would I do it again?

I'm writing this on my new notebook computer, sitting in first class flying to Boston where I'll make personal appearances, sign books and autographs, and appear on the local talk shows on behalf of my next book. Do it again? Of course I'd do it again! It has been, and will continue to be, worth every minute and every effort I spent.

But enough about me. What about *you*? What are you going to get out of all this? A whole bunch about what brilliant things I did to get to be so wonderful? Naaah! While that might sound pretty good to me, my publisher wouldn't think it was such a swell idea, and you'd never recommend this book to your writing group. So, no, you won't get a puff piece on how I made it big in book writing.

What I'd like to show you is how to *think* about publicizing your book, how to *approach* getting publicity, what to expect, and what to look out for.

I will use what I did as example because that's what worked for me, and that's what I know about. I didn't interview thousands of book publicists because, first, I don't know any. (Though I hope soon to get a book contract with one or two of them built in.) And secondly, because what I want to share with you is what you can do *by yourself*. Without a huge budget. And without a lot of cooperation from your publisher.

At the end of this little offering, you should be able to figure out for yourself how to stir up a little noise about the publication of your hard slaved-over tome, and you should understand a little better why it isn't necessary to be interviewed by Dan Rather, Tom Brokaw, or Connie Chung to make the kind of news that sells books.

2
Breaking Through.

Most authors look at publicity as a high wall with a hidden doorway. They think that only the extremely lucky, the extremely powerful, or the extremely well-connected get the kind of publicity that any book needs. And yes, all three of those do get special consideration. That's just the way the world works. But they are not the only ones who can get important space or airtime. So can you. You just have to adjust the way you think about *access*.

The fact is, that every newspaper or magazine starts its daily, weekly, or monthly life as a series of blank pages needing something to fill them. Every radio show is hours of silent airtime looking for interesting topics to talk about. And TV, the toughest of all publicity to get, is still a screen full of snow until some producer, somewhere, figures out what subjects will make exciting or intriguing segments.

Once you begin to accept this view of the media, you begin to understand precisely what it is that will get you and your book welcomed as a feature story, an hour of talk time, or a six-minute section of the nightly newsmagazine.

Cracking the national TV talk shows, while a much more difficult task, is really just an extension of the same principle. Getting on one is *not* impossible to accomplish. It's just that you are up against much greater odds, a huge book-selling competition, and the pro publicist who has an uncle in the control room. Or who, last year, was able to secure Menachem Begin or Fergi as guests, and who is owed early consideration by the show's producers. The Oprah/Donahue arena is a specialized area so valuable to book sellers that we'll give it its own chapter.

Now that you've begun to alter your perception of the media from huge, impenetrable fortresses with guarded gates, to hungry beasts in need of constant feeding, you've accomplished the first and most critical task in getting your book the publicity it needs to succeed—you understand the media's problem.

All you have to do next is figure out how you, and your book, can be part of the solution.

3
The Title Tells The Tale.

While the media *is* constantly hunting for sufficient subjects, competition for attention is fierce. An editor's or producer's time is flush with head-on deadlines, meetings, and appointments. Producers and editors almost never just casually invite you over for a leisurely chat about your book's contents, its history, or its impact on the known and future universe. They rely on publicity people to let them know what and who is available. One thing I'll bet on, since you're reading this book, is that you don't have a huge publicity mill grinding its best on your behalf. Which also means that producers and editors aren't scanning the white pages to see if you're listed. *You* are the one who has to do the calling.

If you're lucky, an actual person may answer a phone and take a message. It's much more likely that you'll get a voice mail service. In either case, you'll have slightly less than a minute and a half to be convincing. And the plain fact is that you're going to get more response with a book titled *Sex In The Year 2000* than with one called *123 New Ways to Wind Your Garden Hose.*

Now it *is* possible to get publicity for the *123 Ways*—just as it is possible to get publicity for any book—*if* you know how to choose your audience. Surely "The Gardening Hour" would be more interested in a book like that than an offering on Kama Sutra future variations. But, *even* the garden show is choosing between a guest who wrote about watering techniques and an author who offers *Stop Killing Your Roses!* So, given a choice between titling your tome *A New Twist on Watering Techniques* or *Let My Plants Live!*, always, always, always *choose the one that you think will be the most intriguing in a one-minute message to the producer of a TV or radio show.*

The offshoot of this kind of decision-making is that, very often, the title you come up with will also be intriguing to a book buying audience. It's a double whammy that you can perform in your own favor. And if the title doesn't completely tell the tale, so what? Give it a subtitle: *Hey Mom, Guess What! (150 Ways To Tell Your Mother You're Gay or Lesbian).* Or *What To Do With A Liberated Woman (A New Etiquette Primer For Men.)*

What if your book is already titled? Some things you can't change. But the strategy is the same. If your book title isn't so outrageous as to give you an instant call back, perfect your one-minute message technique. Make certain that whatever you say to the receptionist, real or electronic, conveys the idea that what you have to say on your book's subject is fascinating, controversial, entertaining, or so unique that someone just *has* to get back to you to set up a booking.

This is tougher to do with fiction, but the concept holds. Title your novel to give you maximum thrust in a one-minute message. Or find a concise way to encapsulate your tale in a fascinating fashion. Or find the news or the noise in your epic.

News or Noise? What do I mean by that? ...Stay tuned.

4
Make News...

Media buys the *different*. It laps up the *odd*. It is addicted to the *new* in the news.

So, without exception, if you want publicity, that's what you have to find in your book.

This concept and your ability to grasp it are the most important things I can share with you. *The newsworthiness of your book is the principle selling tool you have.* I'm not talking about selling your book to the book-buying public, I'm talking about selling yourself, and your book as a story subject, as an interesting hour of radio talk time, or three to six TV minutes.

But what if you don't have access to the secret diaries of Lee Harvey Oswald? What if you don't know anything about David Letterman's sex life? How are you going to find the news in fiction? Or a romance novel?

Again, it's a matter of perspective. Somewhere there is an audience for whom your subject is fascinating. Otherwise your publisher wouldn't have bought the manuscript in the first place. You wrote your book on a silent bet with yourself that someone else would pay for the privilege of reading your mind. Same thing for your publisher. What premise or writing concept does your book have that has never been put forth publicly before. And, most importantly, *who* is it news to?

The first and most potentially rewarding question is: *Is this mainstream news?* If the honest answer is yes, you should be in PR heaven. All you have to do is get word to the media that you have a new story to be told and the doors should begin opening. However, what's news to you may not be new to Sally Jesse's producers, especially given the lag time between when you first got the idea for your book and when you held the first copy.

So you want to know just exactly what it is about your book that makes it *currently* newsworthy in the mainstream.

The next level of news audience to consider is the *specialized markets*. If not everybody, then *who* will be thrilled to know what you did? A book suggesting the existence of a small undiscovered planet orbiting the earth just out of sight behind the moon might make the mainstream, but due to its crank and crackpot potential, it also might fall by the wayside except for the Astrological Society. Or the Science Fiction Society. Both of which might be available to publicize or purchase your book. So you need to find out if groups appropriate to your topic have a newsletter or a radio show. Do they accept speakers for their conventions? And you need to investigate the category's specialty magazines and newspapers.

Every group has specialty publications. Bowlers' Monthly. Dry Cleaners' Digest. Gardeners' Gazette. You name it, there are probably multiple publications catering to its needs and interests. *Your* needs and interests, if you have written something for a specialty market. There are, for example, gay and lesbian newspapers, unknown to the general public, in nearly every city in the country. It's an uncoordinated, unconnected network which provides access to the very people I want to know that I have a new book. I make a special effort to be in contact with as many of these as I can, and to get a copy of the new book into the hands of everyone in my market who could conceivably get it reviewed, preferably in time for the holiday shopping season. By the way, it's no accident that my Christmas Stocking-sized, Garfield-shaped, humor book is released in November. It's a bit of timing I asked the publisher for. She had to do some slight contortions to accomplish it, but that proved to be a successful marketing strategy. So she'll do it again next year. I just *acted as if* I had the right to ask for what was in the best interests of my own book. (An attitude so important to your future success that we'll talk more about in the chapter on what to expect from your publisher.) I was lucky enough to find a receptive listener. You may not be. Some publishers keep total control of such matters and will not listen to your requests, even in the face of extremely strong sales logic. That, however, shouldn't stop you from asking.

But back to the news. Sometimes the news is not in the writing but in the writer. Who besides your nana will be excited and interested to know that you have a published book? Your hometown paper is a good place to start. The national society for which you are the local vice president, perhaps? How about the industry you've been toiling in for the last couple of decades? Would they be willing to publish an announcement? Well, don't just sit there reading...find out!

Now, maybe it isn't in the writer. Maybe your news is in the details of the printing. Is it the first book ever to be printed on paper guaranteed till the third millennium? Was it printed on a reproduction of the press that first printed the Gutenberg Bible? Was chapter one first released on T-shirts given away free with twenty dollars worth of groceries. Is there a one hundred thousand dollar prize for solving the mystery? What's the news that will make the media, and therefore the book-buying public, lift an eyebrow and take notice?

Somewhere, to some audience, you or your book is news. Once you've determined just what news it is, and to whom, then your publicity campaign can begin.

5
...Or Make Noise.

And then there's *Noise*!

You're going to know very quickly if there's no promotable news in your book. You'll know by the enormous, overwhelming silence when you contact program directors, producers, and editors. The deafening sounds of yawning when you propose a program. It may be the news is very similar to what's already out there. Or even that, though newsworthy, your book, or the news you think is in it, is not quite *controversial* enough to move a producer, even in your own hometown, to book you on the afternoon chat show. **THAT'S WHEN YOU NEED TO MAKE SOME NOISE!**

Noise is anything you can think of to get you on the news. It has to be something that a program director can send a camera crew to cover on a slow news day. The world's biggest bake sale? Three hundred acrobats balancing on one chair? Digging the deepest hole in the state? Could be. It could also be a symposium, a concert, a record breaker, or the extraordinary way you have trained your dog to sing. Whatever it is, however, it must be relevant to the book you are trying to publicize.

Suppose you have written *Self-Help For The Popcorn Addicted*. An attention-getting device might be to create a popcorn-a-thon in which the local high school raises money by attempting to top the state record for amount of popcorn popped in one day by a local high school. Or the amount consumed. Or used to pack Christmas presents for the needy. It's a natural for the local paper to cover. And as for the six o'clock TV news, well, the photo ops abound. All you have to do is see that the news desks are notified in time to catch the best action. How hard is that? Pick up a phone, call the local paper or papers and the local or affiliate TV stations, and ask for the news desk. Then hope that on that day no one gets a successful brain transplant or conquers the Western Hemisphere.

Make News! Make Noise!

You have to work a little harder to make noise, because noise events aren't naturally occurring. But you *can* create interesting occurrences that attract mini-cams on slow news days. All they need to be is relevant to your book, interesting, and photogenic or telegenic. Of course you, the celebrity author, are on hand to lend encouragement and to sign autographs or copies of your book, which you either hold up during interviews, or which are prominently displayed around you any time you are on camera.

Chain yourself to a tree? Marry the President's eligible daughter? Build an ergonomically correct house out of bottle caps? Sure. Whatever you can think of to get positive attention is a positive. And when they ask for your name, be sure to add, author of *There's Bucks In Your Buick*. It's a logical extension of the PT Barnum axiom (no, not "There's a sucker born every minute.") that says, "Say anything you want about me, just spell my name right." In this case, it's amended to "Just spell the name of my book right."

Do I recommend that you go out and rob a bank to get your name in the paper? Absolutely not! Nor any other illegal nor unlawful activity. However, Should you find yourself in the unenviable position of being cuffed and dragged bodily into a paddy wagon in public view of a TV crew or reporters, be sure a copy of your book conveniently falls from your jacket pocket in front of the camera. A lot of the secret to being successful at this publicity game is in recognizing your opportunities, and seizing them. Carpe Videocam!

Now here's the complicated part. Once you've made noise, that's *news*!

If you are trying to book yourself onto a radio or TV show or get feature story interest from newspapers and periodicals, what may be of interest to the editors and/or producers is the noise that you made. Now you are no longer merely the author of *Don't Let Football Intercept Your Marriage*. You are the author who perpetrated the skydiving incident in the middle of the third quarter at the Super Bowl.

6
What To Expect From Your Publisher.

Not much. Even from the kindest of them.

If your book is in particular favor or if they paid a lot of advance money, you can expect some help. But most publishers aren't paying for the privilege anymore. So smaller or non-existent advances are the all-too-often norm. And the thought of having to shell out extra to promote books by unknowns seems much too risky for the big houses, and too much additional expense for the smaller ones. If anything, publishers are looking for books by authors who can take themselves a long way. That's probably why they sent you this book or suggested you find it for yourself.

"So why do publishing houses pay publicists for the biggies?" you may well be asking. Simple. Publishing houses are looking for easy income, the most return for the least amount of expended effort. (Aren't we all?) With a known quantity, just about all you have to do is let an author's followers know that there's a new volume, and the bucks pour in. So it's not unheard of for a new Robert Ludlum book to warrant a hundred thousand dollar publicity campaign. The net return on that kind of investment is many millions. The money spent to educate your audience on the existence of *Raising Chameleons For A Healthy Profit* might not result even in paying back the cost of the telephone calls to television stations, much less justify a round trip ticket in cattle car class to Omaha to get you to speak at the Chameleon Breeders' National Convention. (Which you should go to, by the way, if you can afford to get there yourself, and you can get accepted as a speaker.)

Publishing houses are in business to sell books. They know that publicity *does* sell them. They often do allow *something* for publicity on some books. They can often be persuaded to support a sound promotion plan, provided that they don't have to A) *do* too much or B) *spend* too much. Which places the burden of your book's success squarely on the shoulders of your own imagination and initiative.

(About that paragraph in your contract that says that they will do what is reasonable to promote your book... Literal translations: damn little, and never enough. Don't, however, hurry to punch up the office number of your lawyers. Even the most carefully scrutinized contract gives the publishing house the widest latitude.)

There are some things you need to find out from them *before* your book clears the printing company. You want to ask your editor what the publicity plans for your book are. Don't tell him or her that you don't expect him or her to do much of anything except maybe ship books to your local bookstore for a hometown signing if you're lucky. Don't say "*Are* there promotion plans?" That's a dead giveaway that you don't expect anything.

One of the techniques that I expect you to master over the course of this mini course in book PR is one I talked about earlier. It's called, "*Act As If.*" It means that you act as if what you wanted were true. It's an old pop-psychology technique which adapts extremely well to making your book happen the way you want it to.

You will be surprised how often *Acting As If* will get you what you are after. For example, *Act As If*...the publisher is of course going to...spend money and time on you and your book...see that your book is shipped to the cities you are appearing in...reimburse you for at least some of the expenses you are going to incur if you want more people than your high school journalism club to even know that you finally finished your Great American work.

You should also begin immediately *Acting As If*...your book is already a bestseller...people are excited about your imminent arrival at any gathering based on your authordom...bookstores are already lining up to order the next book you issue. This is more than just an exercise in positive mental attitude, it is an absolutely critical step in getting your publisher and everyone else to take you seriously about your book promotion.

Interestingly enough, it is often at smaller publishers that you can get the most promotion mileage. In the big houses, the rules are set. Only certain authors and certain offerings get "A" level treatment. B, C, D, and E treatment are assigned by secret codes you're never likely to crack. The advantage of being published by a big house is that its reputation and distribution do work in your favor, and if you can prove yourself, its publicity department can too. However, in a small house, each book is a carefully considered gamble, staking some of the house's future on its success. While small houses may not have as much money to toss around on your behalf, if they do have any, and you can demonstrate that you can make their money pay off for them, there's a much better chance that you'll actually get some.

But not unless you ask. And not until you clearly determine before publication date specifically what they have in mind for you, can you determine just how much you want to supplement it.

At very least, you should get them to agree to supply you with promotional copies. "Promo" copies are the ones that you give to editors, producers, free-lance reporters, anyone who could get your book reviewed or schedule you on the air. These aren't the copies you give to your Aunt Rose on her seventy-fifth birthday to prove that you could get a book published. Promo copies are in addition to the ten free copies you have coming from your contract. You shouldn't have to pay for them, but you will have to account for them.

My publisher sends me an invoice for all the copies shipped to me. I get a bill at the standard forty percent discount. But then we do a negative accounting. I keep track of every promo or publicity copy I send to a radio station, TV producer, or publication, report the number and destination to the publisher, and the number is subtracted from the total I theoretically owe. If I sell some at an appearance, I send a check for sixty percent of the book's cover price times the number of copies sold. And I also always buy a couple of dozen at my discount so I have treasured cheap gifts to give to non-media people I think deserve an autographed copy.

It isn't that your publisher is mean and stingy or controlling, although since I haven't met your publisher, perhaps s/he is. It's just that most publishers think that just publishing you was risk enough. You are an unknown quantity. Till you can prove yourself, or rather, till your books can prove themselves in the marketplace, betting actual money in the form of a decent sized publicity budget is a long-shot. It's up to you to prove that you can lower the odds.

Now, let's not paint this picture of publishers entirely dark. There are some very positive things that publishers *will* do on your book's behalf. For example, it isn't unusual for a hundred or more copies of your book to be sent out to the media for review. Often you'll get some kind of advertising for the book. Many publishers will not leave your effort to fend entirely for itself, they will do direct mail pieces to specialty markets or prescreened mailing lists. They'll send press releases. Your publisher, like all publishers, wants the best for your book. Because that's also what's best for the publishing house. And the more you can get from the publisher, the better off your book and your bank account will be. The drawback, however is that in any publishing house, there are many babies to tend.

So if you are really determined to make your book successful, you will still have to tend to it yourself. Because no one has the vested self-interest in your book that you do. So what do you do? Well, that's what you came to this book for, isn't it?

7
Do Not Go Naked Into That Good Fight.

Just as no soldier would head into the Sudan without his HumVee, you don't want to head into the battle for attention without the survival gear you need to make a difference in your own life.

There are some things you'll need to have, some things you'll need to do, and some things you'll need to find out.

First you'll need some copies of your own book. We've already talked about how to get them from your publisher with a negative accounting, so you only pay for whatever books you give out for Christmas presents to all the neighbors, charging the rest back to your promotional account. If your publisher won't advance you enough copies of the book, can't afford to send sufficient supplies, or truly believes that the house's publicity department is giving you more than your share, consider buying the discount copies yourself anyway. And sending them out for your own PR. Unless you are a phenomenon, you usually only get one good shot at getting to write books for a living. While the return on *this* book may not justify the cost, figure out the long-term pay back, and make a decision in your own best interest. Naturally, no publishers on this planet will discourage you from spending your own money to promote an enterprise in which they take the higher percentage of the profit.

The next thing you need is one piece of critical information: *Who is distributing your book?*

Contrary to popular belief, neither you nor your publisher is actually in the book-selling business. Bookstores are in the book-selling business. Your job is to see that people want to *buy* from the bookstores, and your publisher's job is to see that easily accessible distributors have enough books to supply those stores.

One of the more important aspects of doing book promotion has to do with direct contact with bookstores and bookstore buyers. When you talk to them, they will all want to know one thing: which distributors are carrying your book. This is how they access their stock. This is how they normally do business. When they ask, they want to know if you are already in the system. Partially because it makes it easier for them. And partially because it verifies for them that you are somehow more legitimate than authors who are printing their books on HP laser printers in their home offices or copy machines at Office Max.

Bookstores don't need phone numbers or addresses. They already have those. They just want to know who to order from. Not knowing is tantamount to admitting that it's your first book, that you don't really know the business, and that maybe *nobody* is distributing, that maybe it is the dreaded *self-published* book, and therefore worthy of less consideration. If, by the way, your book is self-published, then you'll really want to invest in the promotion techniques I'm suggesting, and any other ones you can think of. Getting a self-published book into wide distribution is an art form in itself.

I found it helpful to create a PR BOOSTER KIT for each book. This stays in my possession and when I have an appointment, or am traveling and dropping in on radio or TV stations, major metropolitan dailies, specialty pubs, or bookstores, I always take it along. It shortcuts the process of getting people I am targeting to pay attention.

Here's what it is, and what's in it:

It's a brightly colored zippered three-ring binder with plastic sheet protectors.

The first page has a *copy of the book cover* which your publisher should be able to supply you at no charge. I also keep some of these in the back pocket of the binder for bookstores that can use them for displays, and for print media that can shoot pictures of the flat cover more easily than shooting pictures of the book itself. Right after the book cover page, I have *the book's very best and/or most impressive review*. It could just be a very good review with a swell headline like: "This is the funniest, coolest book ever released!" Or it could just be from some place impressive. I was lucky enough to have a story on *The Dyke Detector* appear in the *Ft. Lauderdale Sun Sentinel*, my hometown paper. The story was picked up by the Associated Press, and sent out on the wire. It was picked up by the *Chicago Tribune*, among other papers, so, naturally, the first masthead and review in my boast book is that one. I follow it up with the best of the rest. No more than *three to five of the choicest reviews*. I figure, by then, I'll have their attention.

Next is a page with large type announcing which *distributors* carry the book. Media won't care about this, so when I'm using it with an editor or producer, I just flip past this page.

Since I write a syndicated biweekly column for a number of papers across the country, I've included some *samples of my work*, with mastheads. Not because I expect anybody looking at the booster book to read them, but because it tells bookstore people, as well as media, that I might have a following who would be interested in what I have to say, or in buying the book. If you have *credentials appropriate to your book's subject* matter, find a way to include them in your PR kit. *411 Delicious Things To Do With Buttered Toast And Not Get Arrested* will carry a little more impressive weight if a copy of your diploma from the Julia Child's Crostini Academy is included.

In the side pocket, besides the extra covers, I also keep *order forms.* Since I try to travel with copies of the book wherever I go, I try to place an immediate seed order of three to five books with any bookstore I encounter. I don't make any money on this, but it gets the book into the store, and that's my goal. The invoice I leave with the bookstore goes into their "30 Day Net" file, which the bookkeeper pays directly to the publisher on or before thirty days from the date of the sale. I make a copy for my own records, and a copy for the publisher. (Usually it will be a carbonless multi-part form anyway.) If the publisher doesn't receive payment, then the publisher's collection department (or secretary) contacts the store, and I am mercifully out of that loop. (NOTE: Before you place seed orders, clear it with your publisher!)

If your book makes any of the *bestseller lists*—distributor's, bookstore's, specialty market's, *New York Times',* anyone's—keep a copy of that in the kit as well.

Include anything that makes the book look desirable to a bookstore buyer, and that makes you seem fabulously interesting to the media.

Remember, your boast book is a sales tool. It can say all the things that are hard for you to say out loud without seeming like you think you're heaven's gift to the modern written word. There are plenty of times when I just leave the kit in the car. But when I need a little assistance in touting my tome, I just haul it out and say, "If you have a minute or two, I'd like to show you a book you ought to know about."

8
There's A Difference Between Ego And Business.

If you're any good at all at this, some of your soon to be ex-friends will accuse you of being very good at self-promotion. They will not necessarily mean it as a compliment, which doesn't mean you shouldn't take it that way. And be perfectly willing to share the secrets of *your* success should *they* ever reach the exalted state of publication that you have accomplished. The plain fact is that folks will treat you differently upon publication, and the distance will grow greater as the book's success increases.

Now why, you may be wondering, would I want to bring up how your friends and ex-friends treat you in a book about getting publicity?

Well, a lot of the work of getting people to know about your book will seem like self-involved, ego aggrandizement to those people. And some of it will seem like that to you too.

It's an obstacle. *Get over it.*

While a lot of the activity of book promotion will, as an after-effect, be ego boosting, the mere fact of your getting to do it, is the business you need to be about. Talking on the radio for an hour in your hometown will make you a little more well known among your friends. *Ego.* It will also let perfect strangers know that you have a book that they might be interested in looking for, and maybe even spending their hard-won cash on. *Business.*

Signing your name in the flyleaf is a lot like giving autographs. *Ego. Ego. Ego.* Well, signed books are more valuable, and sell faster in a store than unsigned ones. They draw people to look at the book in the first place, people who might not take the trouble to sort through the shelves. *Business. Business. Business.*

And TV, well, my oh my. I once had some completely separate business to do with the owner of a posh and popular restaurant cafe. In the course of our conversation, the title of the book came up. The woman who had not been paying particular attention to me other than as a kind of necessary business nuisance, stopped for a full few seconds, looked intently into my face and proclaimed loudly, "I saw you on TV! You had that book! I bought it for my sister!" The ego, not to mention an elegantly prepared and attentively served luncheon, got served that day. *Ego.* But the fact that she had bought the book was the *business* I was about when I did the TV interview she had seen.

So what's the point? Easy. When it comes to this kind of promotion, you really have to stuff your ego in a suitcase you will unpack later. You also have to pack away your own modesty. Who is going to rush out to their nearest local bookstore to demand a copy of anything you touted as merely "kinda, aw shucks, pretty good?" Nobody. But if you can manage to get them to think that it is the hottest thing since Leggo my Eggo, well, then, you can probably start yourself a sales avalanche.

9
Baiting Hooks.

Fishing always seemed to me to be one of those impractical sports that left a thing or two to be desired in the productive results category. If you're secretly seeking an opportunity to stand solitary in cold water wearing rubber, okay, then you can get your goal accomplished easily. But if you have only one pole, one line, one hook, and one worm, and you're hoping for dinner, then you'd best be darn certain that whatever gods may be have your best dining interests at heart.

If, on the other hand, you have a hundred poles, a big pile of cheese balls, and a whole lot of hooks in the water at any given time, then your chances of eating are significantly improved.

Getting publicity is exactly the same. If you are counting on any one source or resource, you could find yourself skipping some servings. But enough metaphors. At least enough of this one for a while. The idea of dealing in multiple opportunities and working on a percentage basis is a *press for success* principle probably first used by chariot salesmen. It makes sense for you too.

You just can't count on any one source of publicity coming through. It's too hard on the stomach lining unless you're a practicing masochist. What you have to do is send out your stuff in waves big enough so that one or two have a chance of coming back in your favor. Don't just contact a local radio show and hope that the host bites. Don't send one copy of your work to the local paper hoping for a rave review, or any review at all. *Send your stuff everywhere.*

We'll get to the specifics of exactly how to approach different types of media in a minute. But for now, suffice it to say, you need to operate on the *more is not less principle.* If there are three papers in your area, or six in seven nearby counties, send something to each and every one of them.

Contact the producer of every radio and TV show for which your subject would be appropriate. Call them. Send them letters. Let them get used to your name. And don't just do it once, do it whenever there is a legitimate occasion to do so.

Let me just add a word about disappointment here. If you count too much on any one source, you can get very frustrated. On my last trip out for *Hey Mom, Guess What!,* the book that followed *The Dyke Detector,* I talked to the assistant book editor of a big paper in a big town I was visiting on other business. She passed me on to a reporter whose interest I gauged in the seven to eight out of ten range. Based on that, I scurried over with a review copy and my biggest, most sincere smile. The reporter was pleasant, gracious, and apparently very interested. She was leaving, she said, for the Thanksgiving holiday, and would return on Monday. "Okay," I replied. "I'll call you then."

"In the bag" I thought, and as a result didn't pursue the smaller, cross town rival. Why tick off the city's biggest paper by going to the competition? It made sense at the time, but I forgot my own guidelines.

On Monday, the reporter wasn't at her desk. Overdose of white foods, I wondered? Perhaps she was in a train wreck. I called eight times that day. I also called the next day. And the next. Now I don't suppose that she was specifically staying away from her desk on the off chance that when she picked up the phone it would be me and she'd have to tell me that she hated what I had written. I think that something else came up.

But I made the mistake of banking on her positive response, and so far have not gotten my name in her paper. Maybe she really did hate the work. Maybe she was too busy to tell me. Or maybe she was just too busy, and will think of me at some time in the future. All I know is that after the sixth or seventh call on the second and third days with no response (I only left a message or two a day with my location and phone numbers) I knew that I just might be beginning to sound a tad desperate...Not *ever* a recommended posture when you're seeking publicity...and that it would be in my best interest to just let it go.

My time would have been better spent calling *all* the papers in the area — the two majors, and all the appropriate neighborhood throwaways and weekly shoppers to see what interest I could drum up in the short time I had available. I should have pursued any and all that showed the slightest blip on their EEGs about talking to me.

When it comes to securing publicity from any medium, the watch words have to be:

- *Nothing ventured, nothing gained.*
- *If you don't ask, you don't get.*
- *Don't put all your eggs in one basket.*
- *Que sera, sera.*
- *C'est la goddamn vie.*
- *Next!*

10
All The News That Fits In Print.

Let's Start With The Biggies.

Without any news, any noise, or any luck, it is nearly impossible to get a major metropolitan daily to do your story. We can't do much about your luck, but you've already learned how to find the news or make the noise.

Your next step in getting your name in the paper is to locate a resource readily available to you. The paper. It's probably on the nearest corner in a coin box. Or on your front porch this very minute. You can find all kinds of helpful information there. The name of the Executive Editor, Editor-In-Chief, Feature Editor, Lifestyle Editor, Regional and/or Metro Editor, and, of course, the Book Editor. These are your targets. They are usually not very accessible, but that shouldn't stop you from trying. Try calling the paper and asking for them by name. You may get through, and you're on your way. Just give them the one-minute pitch and see what happens. The secretarial screen at papers is pretty high though. You probably won't get through on the first try, but it's worth a shot.

When I'm tackling a major metropolitan daily where I don't know anybody, I've found it much better just to get in the car with a stack of books and brown envelopes. I usually only get as far as the guard. I hand over my envelopes, which 1) are addressed by name or nickname—Rich, instead of Richard J.—if that's the way he's generally known, 2) contain a book that's autographed to the specific editor, and, most importantly, 3) include a very short letter outlining an appropriate slant for a story on my book. It is different for each editor.

If there *is* a hard news story, that's what goes in the letter to the Editor or Executive Editor. If I can't find a hard news connection, then I usually just try to figure out some advantage to the paper, let the editor know that I'm a subscriber if I am, or a regular reader (even if I'm not), and ask for the courtesy of having the editor pass the book on to the appropriate person. This is a low probability ploy. But on the *baiting hooks* theory, I figure it only costs the publisher a buck or two for the extra book if nothing happens. But if my book and story slant manage to snag the attention of the key editor, usually I'll get a story in the paper. It's a high odds gamble I think is worth taking.

For the Metro/Lifestyle or Feature or Regional Editor, the letter usually offers a couple of suggestions for story angles around the book. Just bare outlines, or pointers. It's important not to write the whole story because it insults the editor you're trying to woo. Sometimes for the Metro or Regional Editor, I offer the Local-author-makes-good approach with appropriate "look what has happened to *this* book" information as the story. It is great publicity if the paper runs a big, splashy, color picture of your book's cover, and an interview on your views, perspectives, and details of daily living. But it is also nearly as valuable if the paper runs a story on how, for example, to replace roof tiles beautifully and economically with discarded aluminum cans, and quotes you, by name, from your newly released manual: *Save Cash! Use Trash!*

You Can't Make Book On The Book Editor.

Surprisingly, the editor you're the least likely to do well with is the Book Editor. S/he is inundated daily, and has three hundred running feet of autographed books at any given time that never, ever, see the light of newsprint. You usually don't have a great slant to offer a book editor other than that your book exists. Unless you can catch his or her fancy, well, there's one promo copy you can be thankful the publisher is paying for. However, if your book has made any of the bestseller lists we previously mentioned, if a local organization, or if, oh, say, The National Book or Pulitzer Committees, have recognized the work as particularly laudable, you may have a chance at a mention or an article. Also, if something odd happened in the printing, distributing, or promotion of the book (a crate of your books fell from a Federal Express plane, landing at the edge of a frozen lake at the hands of a child who had fallen through the ice, and your book is credited with the rescue) then that's the information you want to pass on to the Book Editor. Remember, it isn't the Book Editor's job to flack your book. His or her purpose in life is to steer readers to little known tomes worth their time (for whatever reasons); to let readers in on the latest and the best in books; and to head them away from content-free offerings with major promo budgets. If you can tie your book into any one of those efforts, you can probably make a friend of the book editor, and you may be able to get a quotable review out of it.

Notice that I said a "quotable" review. Book reviews are usually buried in the paper, and are read by people who look for them specifically, as opposed to a general information article which can reach nearly everybody with a paper in his/her hands. So, while a review has a limited immediate effect, it's not the best way to reach a wide audience.

However.

There's nothing to stop you from taking what's good in the review, and clipping a quote:

"Wicked funny!"
—*Miami Herald*

and putting it in very large type at the beginning of your Boast Book. There's nothing wrong with telling the TV producer that the Roanoake Herald said the book was brilliant (if they actually did say that.) Or exclaiming loudly in your press release, or on radio and television how humbled you are that the Dallas Gazette Or Omaha Clarion thought your book was "the reason they invented printing." Find a way to work the best of the reviews into whatever else you are doing. This is one of those business vs. ego situations.

By the way, if they didn't give you a rave, take a lesson from the movies which can turn a review that actually said "If this is great acting, I'm a polka dot rhinoceros. Do not put this on your list of movies you have to see this year!" into a promo that screams:

Great acting....
...Put this on your list of movies you have to see this year!

Even in the worst review, there is a probably a quotable nugget that, right after you go through a box of Kleenex or a case of something inebriating, can be extrapolated and quoted in your next promo opportunity.

While we're still talking about Gotham City's Daily Planet, there's another group of newspaper people you want to consider approaching about your book. *The Columnists.* If there is a way you can tie your work into what they are writing, by all means call up the paper, ask for the columnist—who will usually take your call—and announce yourself as the author of a book that is right up his/her alley. Then get into your car and deliver the autographed copy that day, or call a courier and get it over to the paper ASAP. Columnists have notoriously short attention spans. This is a real baited hook. But if the columnist bites, you've got a mention in a column that some group of readers turns to on purpose. You can put it into your Boast Book, and/or tell your future contacts that the columnist over at the *Record* mentioned you just the other day.

Approach weekly, biweekly, monthly, and quarterly mainstream publications exactly the same way.

Once you get to know the editors, you may be able to take a more personal approach. Just because they know you better. Now that I have met, worked with, and know many editors and reporters, they'll take my calls easily. They've had some experience with me. They know I'm good for a story, and I don't have to work nearly so hard to get their attention. If you can establish a connection that is a personal/professional one, it will go a very long way toward getting you the publicity your next book needs. I found the initial barriers at city newspapers and major publications among the toughest to get through when I was just starting out, but if you don't give up, it does get easier.

Going National.

It would be really nice to be able to sit at home and attract national newspaper coverage. It is possible, but both difficult and unlikely. Being there is always better than "long distance" for newspapers unless you really do have news of national import.

Whenever you are in a new town with a dozen copies of your book, (*Don't leave home without them!*) you should always try the same I'm-just-in-from-out-of-town approach for newspapers that I detail in the next chapter for away-from-home radio stations. The worst they can say is "No" and if they say "Yes" it's a real bonus.

Trying to get their attention from your house is hard. You can create a national print mailing list for yourself, and send out books and letters which detail your story angle. Without a personal connection, a compelling reason to feature you in their pages, or an obvious way to link you to their readership, most papers in cities other than where you live will pass.

It's too much work making it into the national dailies. Particularly because you have to catch them one paper at a time. I don't think that kind of fishing is really worth the work when I look at the rewards of spending my time generating other kinds of publicity. But you have to make that decision for yourself.

Making It Into The Mags

Time, *Newsweek*, and the general interest magazines are certainly worth a letter and a copy of the book. But they are long shots. Most likely, they will feature you and your book only after you have been successful with all the other publicity efforts, and by the time that happens, they'll be pursuing you, so you don't have to waste your efforts. But aiming high never hurts, so find the news in your book and slap some stamps on an envelope. Don't bet the ranch on a feature story. Just hope that they have a story in mind already, that might be better with a tiny color copy of your book featured in a sidebar column. Look at it this way, *if they don't have a copy of your book, they can't even consider giving you a mention.*

Serving The Special Interests

Special interest publications really *are* worth your while. They cater to audiences that are prescreened for you. If your book is appropriate for them, then your inclusion as a feature, a review, or a short recommendation is much easier to attain.

Get to the biggest branch of your local library you can find, and make friends with the reference librarian. S/he can hand you the books that list the publications by interest as well as circulation. (Several of which are listed at the end of this chapter.) These directories will give you addresses, phone numbers, and the names of senior and special editors. Be careful of the names. Since most of the directories are compiled only once or twice a year, the personnel information may not be current. If you find some prime targets, it might be worth the AT&T investment to the publication's telephone operator to ask for the name and spelling of the editor of the department you think might be most receptive. If it's a small publication, go ahead and ask to be put through and make your best one-minute pitch. If you don't ask, they've already said, "No."

What Did You Say?

You will be misquoted somewhere in any print story. You can count on it. Don't panic. Don't write letters to the editor unless the misquote is libelous (in which case, the letter you want to write is to your lawyer), or unless the misinformation is life or death to someone else. Remember Barnum, and hope they either spell your name right, or at least get the book title close enough so a book clerk can figure out what an intrigued customer is actually asking for.

Do It Yourself.

Another way to give yourself some extra publicity trades heavily on the fact that you're already a writer. Since you have your nose in these pages, it is probably safe to assume that you have a published, or about to be published, book. These credentials could qualify you to join, as a contributor, the ranks of the very same publications you'd like to be mentioned in.

Offer the publication articles that highlight your work. Use your book as your qualifying credential. Or become a columnist. Columnists always, or almost always get a closing signature that identifies them at the bottom of their columns. You should be identifying yourself as the author of *Fifty Fabulous Outhouse Floorplans* there.

If you already happen to be writing to your market, just change your ID signature to include the new book. And while you're at it, *ask your editors to review your book.*

Print References

To locate some of the mainstream and specialty publications appropriate to your particular market, ask your reference librarian for:

The Gale Directory of Publications and Broadcast Media
Karen Troskynski Thomas & Deborah M. Burk, Editors

Ulrich's International Periodicals Directory
A Reed Reference Publishing Company

Directories in Print-Publishing Section
Charles B. Montney, Editor

Beacon's Publicity Checker
Volume I lists magazines by industry. Volume II lists daily and weekly newspapers. Not all libraries carry these, so you may have to check around or find a friend in an advertising or PR agency who would be willing to loan them to you. You can also buy them. A year's subscription costs $150 + $5. Call 1(800) 621-0561

Radio-TV Interview Reports Publicity Blitz Database
Bradley Communications Corp., P.O. Box 1206, Landsdowne, PA 19050 This is the print arm of a group I'll be recommending later in the radio and TV sections. This one-time database costs $295 plus $40 for the PC compatible or Mac software to run it on, and contains 11,000 newspaper, magazine, and newsletter contacts searchable by name, topic, and city. You can also order this as a subscription with quarterly updates on disk for $445, or as a pre-printed set of mailing labels for $335. This will save you months of research and will probably amortize out over your next several books. I use it. It's gotten me dozens of interviews. I recommend it if you can afford it. For exact information, call 1(800) 989-1400, ext. 703.

11
Radio Daze.

One of the most effective ways to get your book noticed is to get yourself booked on radio talk shows. There are scads of them all over the country, even some in your own hometown, which is the perfect place for you to start. It's not that hard to get yourself on the schedule just as long as you remember the basic premises and principles. First, that the media are giant, hungry gullets needing constant feeding, and secondly, that you and your book have the ability to make news or make noise.

Start by listening to your own radio. Who's on? Who's good? Who's listened to by the most people? There are two advantages to starting your public relations (PR) effort in your own hometown, besides the fact that you don't have to pay for plane tickets, rental cars, or hotel rooms. You're local. And local people who write books are interesting to the other locals, and therefore interesting to the radio talk shows. The stations are all within driving distance, so you can deliver some of your promotional copies directly to the station, and can, without sending your Sprint bill into the stratosphere, call repeatedly until they either give you a hearing or convince you that if you don't stop calling, they'll have you locked up for harassment.

The other advantage you have in your own neighborhood is that you have some idea whether the local talk hosts are friend or foe. For the most part, choose friends. It can make a difference in book sales. People who hear you on the air don't have a clue what your book is like, but if they like you from what they hear, they are often willing to look for your work.

I personally can't stand waiting around for a reply to a letter that might have been "round-filed." So I prefer to phone the station. If I don't know the particular programs on a station (unlikely on my home ground) then I ask for the **Program Director**. The PD is charge of the overall scheduling of a station. And while she or he may not be the one to book you for an hour on Saturday morning, she or he will know who in the line-up is just right. The PD can usually refer you to the right producer or, depending on the size and budget of the station, can be the producer of the show you should be on.

Breaking Through The Screen

What I do when I have learned the PD's name from the receptionist is say "Thank you" and hang up. I give it ten minutes and call back. If you act as if the receptionist is doing you a huge favor to connect you to the PD, or you show a second's hesitation about asking for the connection, the receptionist/secretarial screen will go right up, and you will be told that Mr. or Ms. Jones is tied up in a year-long meeting, but she'll be happy to take a message. "And *whoooo* are you with again?" Get that and you're dead in the water. Don't even bother trying to explain. Just say that you'll call back later, pull up a mirror, and practice your attitude. Then, when you're sure nobody could resist putting your extremely important, yet not 911 urgent, call through, call back.

Act As If Mr. or Ms. Jones would, of course, take your call since you are *The Author* calling—**attitude, not words**—and, more often than not, you'll get through. When I have the PD on the phone, I tell her/him my name and immediately announce a brand new book out or coming out in the next few weeks, called (remember—title, title, title) *Breast Feeding Kills Babies/JFK Was My Mother's Secret Lover/Hitler's Hidden Kitchen Secrets*...and I would *love* to do an interview with _____. Is there any time available on the schedule in the next couple of weeks?

If I know which host(s) I want, I ask for the one I feel most comfortable with. If not, I just say that I would love to be on the station.

If I know, or can find out, the name of the particular producer of the show I want to be on, I ask for her or him first, and bypass the PD entirely. (Often the talk hosts mention the producer's name in the course of a week's programming. It can't hurt to know the show anyway, so listening won't waste your time.) I tell her or him exactly the same thing I would have said to the PD, and I wait a beat to see if there is a flicker if interest. (You can hear it in the breathing.) If there is, I wait to let them woo me onto the station. Occasionally, I actually get booked immediately like this. But mostly only if I know the producer or I have done a show previously on the station and have proved that I can be an interesting guest who prompts telephone calls and generally fills up the airtime. Mostly, however, both the PD and the producer will ask to see the book. Since I work for myself, I prefer to drive a copy over to the station, and have covered a radius of at least fifty miles from my home office to get the copy into the producer's hands. Rarely do I get to see the producer at that point. Usually, I only see the fence guard or receptionist to hand over the envelope with the producer's name on it.

I usually don't call the next day, partially to see if the producer will call me, a highly desirable vantage point for the immediate show and for future bookings for other books, and also because I don't want to appear too eager (read desperate). Most of the time, I just wait a day then call back. Radio people aren't nearly as hard to talk to as TV people, so you can usually get through after the book is at the station. Just tell the receptionist that Mr. Jones is expecting your call.

When you get through, it doesn't hurt to chat up the producer as best you can and as much as he or she and time will allow. Then just ask the question. "What are the chances of getting on X's show before Christmas?" You should get a pretty clear answer. Most producers don't have time to string you along. They'll tell you either yes or no. Sometimes they'll say that they can't do anything now, but that maybe they can get you on in a couple of months. Press. If the producer is just being polite, you want to make them say the words, "No thanks" to you, so you don't hang around helplessly hoping. If, in fact, the producer really means it, make an appointment to call around the indicated time to set a schedule. Don't push to get it scheduled on the spot. Two months is a hundred and three in radio years, so all you'll do is get the producer teed off. Just say, "'Couple of months, huh. Okay, cool. Let me give you a call, oh, say, the first week in February and we can see what's up then." Then put that producer into your daily planner for February and remember to make the call.

Don't be discouraged if it doesn't work on the first producer. Or the fourth. Remember, your PR campaign is based on the baiting hooks philosophy, and the more hooks, the more likely you'll be successful. Each and every producer is important, but each is only one of your many publicity possibilities.

If you do get the producer's interest (and you *can* hear it in the breathing), you want to do everything you can to get yourself booked. Beyond the mere intrigue of my book's title, premise, or newsworthiness, *sometimes I offer show suggestions.* This might mean giving the producer a particular slant that would entertain an audience for an hour or two. It could also mean supplying additional guests. For example, since my books usually break at holiday times, and people often go home to visit family at holiday times, it seemed natural to suggest a show about the traumas that might arise from telling your parents you're gay during the festivities. I gave the producer an idea for a show with just a bit more of a bite, and also suggested a subject that listeners could call in and comment on. On another show that was post-holiday, I could hear the producer's interest losing the battle to his doubt. That was when I suggested that I bring along a gay man whose mother was also a lesbian and a son who not only was out to his mother, but I could also supply the mother. We got *two* hours on the station, an hour more than I expected.

In your own backyard, surely you know some interesting people who won't trip over their own tongues if you invite them to come onto the radio with you. When they are appropriate, suggest interesting people that you can supply (so the producer doesn't have to do any more work) to join you to make an even more interesting show. Just be careful not to bring on any guests who are so extraordinary or articulate, or who have such a fascinating story that they steal the thunder from you and your book. It's a cruel reality, but you are looking for your *own* publicity, not looking to make your friends famous at your book's expense. It's a bit of a tightrope to walk, but one that, when it works, works well.

Selecting the time for your promotional effort can also make a difference. Not just Christmas. You and your book *Making Spreadsheets Make Sense* might stand a better chance for radio airtime if you frame your publicity effort in late March or early April, and offer producers a show on how easy it is to do your taxes out of a shopping bag if you use a computer. *Don't Waste Your Wedding* would get better attention in May than in October. But *The Death Mask Mysteries, The Pumpkin Papers,* or *Full Moons Make You Fat,* all might fare better in October.

You should be thinking like a Program Director. How can you augment your particular story? What angles, guests, or timing will make your story more interesting? Not only radio, but TV and print will often respond when you give them a fuller possibility for using you. Your objective may be to get your book's title mentioned, but the producer's and editor's goal is to have an interesting show, segment, or article. The closer you can get them to their objective, the better your chances of getting publicity.

Out Of Town Is Different.

Never leave home without planning to take advantage of the trip as a publicity opportunity. If you travel on business, have to go see the grandkids in another state, or won round trip airfare to Winter Carnival, you have an entirely different publicity possibility, which could involve all the media, but most likely will pay off on the radio.

When you have advance warning of your itinerary, when you know months or weeks ahead of time that you are going to be in Cleveland for a week or a few days, you can find out the radio stations with the talk meisters, and call or write them to let them know that you're available during a given period of time. Again, I prefer to call, because I don't wait well and the contact is better and more immediate by phone. Sometimes I do fax material into a station, but, unless I already have a contact I've been talking with at the station, I don't think the odds are good enough of landing on the right desk to warrant the assault on my MCI card.

When I call, I just duplicate the local procedures, only early in the conversation, I am very specific about being or coming *in from out of town*, and will *only be available in their area for a limited period*, from x-day to x-day.

I start this story with the secretary or receptionist. I announce myself as *an author* calling to see about scheduling an interview—"Is the Program Director available?"—and usually get my call put through.

Invariably, the out of town producers can't and won't book anything without seeing a copy. Depending on the value of the show to your publicity effort, you can overnight the book with a brief letter, or you can save money and use two- to three-day Priority Mail from the post office. I never, ever, ever, ever, ever use regular mail. Not only because you just can't count on how long it will take, but because the special envelopes that overnight and priority come in always get opened. They just do. It's a law or something.

Anyway, after they have had a day or two to consider your book as a potential talk topic, call them again and see if they'll bite.

Since you are from out of town, you have permission to persist. Sure, they might think of you as a nuisance, but usually you'll get a direct answer from them, and often a booking. Good manners would hardly let you call a fifth time to leave a message. Good publicity, however, wouldn't let you *stop* till you heard from them. If, by the seventh call, you can feel the phone freezing in your hand, move on to your next available target.

And Now, Live, In Our Studio...

Your first time in a studio doesn't have to be quite as traumatic as open heart surgery, though the latter may seem less painful.

When you have secured your booking, the first thing you want to do is listen to the host for a few days, if you have that luxury. That way you'll know whether you have to bring the birth control statistics for Seattle from 1928 through 1934 to defend yourself, or whether you can relax and have fun with your host.

Get to the station a little early. Not an hour ahead, but fifteen or twenty minutes. Radio stations don't have Green Rooms (guest waiting rooms), so there won't be any place for you to wait except in the very public lobby. You know they don't make Marlo Thomas or Alexander Haig wait out there, at least not for long, so you shouldn't either. Of course, That Woman and the General both know enough not to get there too soon, so take your cues from them.

Eventually someone will bring you back to the studio, which is divided into two parts: *The Control Room* and *The Broadcast Booth*. If the station is polite, and doesn't want you to have to wait out in public, someone will find you a chair in the control room till it's time for you to be on the air. The control room is where most of the major knobs and buttons are. At some stations, the producer is also the engineer or *Board Op*. (Short for Operator. The Board is the *Control Board* with all those sliders, buttons, and tape players.)

Just sit where they tell you, and try to relax. Watch what's going on, and get comfortable with the idea that you are going to be on the radio where absolutely nobody you know will be tuned in if you do well, but where everybody you went to high school with will be listening if you screw up. If the board op happens to look up, ask you a question or offer you a cup of the battery acid that masquerades as coffee in most stations, you can consider that permission to talk *very briefly*. Ask how soon you will be going in, where the rest room is, and if you can get a tape of your segment at this time. But only when s/he is not paying rapt attention to something going on with the show. This is not a great time to start a conversation about your favorite use for tequila, or the jerk who gave you the speeding ticket on your way to the studio. The board op is the one who keeps the host on time, makes certain the scheduled commercials and breaks get aired at their assigned time, and signals the host when the station has to break away for network news. S/he will not take kindly to you if you have to be baby-sat when you come into the studio.

If you want a copy of your time on the air (You do!), and you don't have anyone at home taping for you, then bring your own appropriate length blank cassette tape, and give it to the board op when you go into the studio. Stations don't usually provide guests with blank tapes or copies unless you ask, and they often don't even keep their own air check tapes after the broadcast. So if you forget to bring a tape, or want a copy after the fact, forget it.

A few minutes before your assigned time, you will be taken or sent into the studio which might be big enough to park a small semi or small enough to hang up one shirt. The size, furnishing, and equipment all vary. What won't vary is that the host will be on one side of some kind of a console, and you will be on the other. The host is on the side that has microphone buttons and *Cart* players (carts are plastic cartridges about the size of eight-track cassettes that contain short sound effects, sound bites, or favorite bits that the host plays whenever s/he feels like it.)

In front of your chair will be a microphone. It could be round, stick-like, oblong, suspended from above, or anchored to the desk. It could be covered with a dark gray or black foam *sock* that keeps you from sounding like you're spitting into it (even if you are), sounding like a s-s-s-s-s-snake is loose in the studio, or popping your P's. It could be bare silver metal. Long and thin, or short, shiny, and squat. Whatever you find, remember *that microphone is your best friend.* You want to get very close to it. Not close enough to catch infectious germs from the previous guest, but close enough not to sound like you are talking to the audience from the back of a railroad car. *You should be no further than two or three inches away from the microphone when you are talking.*

One thing that people new to the radio studio often fall victim to is looking at the host while they are talking, even if the host is positioned so that doing so it throws them off-mike. I personally believe that that's a nasty trick foisted on innocents by hosts who work for people who saw an inch off the front legs of their office guest chairs. Don't fall for it. You can make all the eye contact you want while s/he is asking the questions. But when it comes time to talk *lean into the mike, and keep an even, comfortable distance. Don't move off-mike, or raise or lower your voice unnaturally* because you will drive the board op nuts. If you are nervous, and your voice changes volume or pitch, the board op is the one who has to worry about making sure you get heard. Just relax and talk as naturally as you can.

One other concern. Many people move their heads from side to side when they converse. It seems natural. It plays hell with the volume level, and even the fastest board op neither can, nor will, expend the effort to keep your sound levels even. Probably s/he will just send some secret let's-dump-this-puppy-quickly signal to the host, and your time will go even faster whether you've had any fun or not. It will seem awkward at first, but *keep your head steady* and your mouth mere inches from the mike, and you'll be just fine. It will get easier the more you do it.

When you're not speaking into the microphone, keep quiet. Totally and completely. Just because you're not on, doesn't mean that your microphone isn't. Even if your mike is turned off, the host's mike can often pick up ambient noises in the studio. Simple rule: Speak when spoken to. Shut up during the rest of the time.

When you are talking, *talk about your book by name.* Your subject matter is fascinating, which is how you got a whole book out of it in the first place. But your business is not to give away the store. Your business is to intrigue your listeners into going into a bookstore to buy your book. I know that seems like a lecture, but you'd be amazed how often authors get so engrossed in being on the radio that they give everything but the title. If the host doesn't do it for you at least once every *segment* (between breaks for commercials) then find a way that isn't too obvious or is humorous to mention your title. It is every publicist's nightmare to get a guest booked on a big radio or TV show like CBS Radio News or the Today Show, then have the author neglect to mention the book's title. *Arghhh!*

You don't have a publicist to remind you to say that your book, *Erotic Horoscopes*, is available at all the local Waldenbooks. Or to say, "Well, Fred, the reason I wrote *351 Ways To Fry An Egg*, answers this caller's question perfectly...." You have *me* to remind you. I just did.

If the producer, engineer, or host offers you a pair of earphones, put them on. Not every station has them, and though they may seem odd to you at first, they are a luxury that's also a great help. The headphones are plugged into the board, and let you hear all of the things that are going out over the air. Not everything that is being broadcast is piped into the studio, so you may not know what is going on. With earphones, you know when a commercial is playing (you can probably talk to the host then, but not much, just to be safe), when they are coming back to you live, and generally where you are in the line-up. I always thought it was rude to have a host who wore phones, but didn't offer me any. He always knew stuff I didn't. Like when he had cut off my microphone. (Oh yes, that has happened on occasion.) I solved that problem for myself with a very big purse (Guys, you look great with a flight bag) inside of which I have a set of my own headphones and a headphone extension cord, both available at your nearest Radio Shack. You need the kind with the big jack (*RCA* plug). The kind that plugs into your Walkman (mini) doesn't work. I don't always pull them out and demand that they plug me into the board, but if the host has them, and I don't, I often ask if there is a spare pair of phones or a guest plug nearby. It isn't necessary, but it is a nicety, and it helps keep me focused on the show.

About the only other thing you need to know is when to leave.

On a normal show, you will leave at the top of the hour when the station cuts away to the news and you are off the air. Thank the host, personalize his or her book if you haven't already, pack up your stuff quietly and go. Pick up your tape from the board op, and hope your mom got to hear you because you sounded so wonderful, the calls were all complimentary, and the host couldn't recommend your book enough.

However.

Sometimes the host is a jerk. Or a bastard. Or a bigot. Or amazingly rude. If things are going very well for the host at your expense, it is always important to remember that while you may feel like you are in a conversation one-on-one with the host, in fact you are really speaking to everyone with half an ear to their radio. Sometimes it is worth the effort just to stay and take on the host. If your debate techniques are up to snuff, or if being humiliated will gain you enough sympathy to interest listeners in finding your book, by all means stay.

If you are the subject of unpleasant attacks, and you don't see any point in continuing your presence, then, just as soon as your mike is turned back on, announce to the audience your intention to leave. Say something extraordinarily polite if you can muster it, like "I can't believe that you subject guests to this kind of unpleasantness in the name of entertainment. My book is called, *Making Up With Your Mother*, and your listeners can find it at their local bookstores. *They* may enjoy listening to this kind of malarkey. *I*, however, have better things to do with my time. I have to darn my socks. Please excuse me." Then get up and go. You may or may not want to stop in the control booth to get your tape. You may just want to leave and let the devil take the hindmost.

In any case, you do want to tune in to the station on your way home to see what nasty things the host has to say about you. It's good publicity. Do not, repeat, *do not take any of this personally*! Lots of radio talk jocks keep their audiences by their outrageousness, and if you got caught, it was because you didn't know any better. On the bright side, confrontation can often keep you and your book on listeners' minds in ways and for lengths that might not have happened if everything was so sweet and gooey that diabetic listeners needed to up their insulin.

Radio References

Here are some ways to find radio talk shows that are easier than booking a flight to every major city in the country or running your phone bill into the ionosphere asking the information operator which are her favorite talk hosts:

<u>Talk Shows & Hosts On Radio</u>, Second Edition by Annie M. Brewer
A Directory of 1052 Radio talk shows and their hosts. Including Show Titles and Formats, Biographical Information on Hosts, and Topic/Subject Index. $32.95 Whiteford Press — Dearborn, Michigan 1(800) 972-2584

<u>Bacon's Radio/TV Directory</u>
Not all libraries carry this, so you may have to check around, or find a friend in an advertising or PR agency willing to let you look. You can also buy them. A year's subscription costs $150 + $5. Call 1(800) 621-0561

<u>Broadcast & Cable Yearbook</u>
Directories in Print-Broadcast Media Section
Charles B. Montney, Editor

<u>Gale Directory of Publications and Broadcast Media</u>
Karen Troskynski Thomas & Deborah M. Burk, Editors

If you have a little more money and you want to do a little less work, here are a couple of other options:

Shelly Roberts' 150 Top Radio Talk Show Choices—culled from all the sources I could find, and several who found me, these shows are my picks in the largest markets.
150 address labels—$15.95. Yearly update—$9.95
IBM compatible ASCII file on 3.5 disk—$24.95. Yearly update—$12.95
Send check or money order to Paradigm Publishing, P.O. Box 3877, San Diego, CA 92102. Florida residents add appropriate sales tax.

TV-Radio Interview Report   Phone: 1(800) 989-1400, ext. 703
Bradley Communications Corp., P.O. Box 1206, Landsdowne, PA 19050
This is a bimonthly "magazine" of 1/4-, 1/2-, and full-page display ads sent to 4,000 radio and TV producers in the United States. A single 1/2-page ad run in 1 issue will cost you $325, and the publisher says that an average expenditure is from $600 to $900. All they need is a copy of your book, a photo, and your check, and they'll write your ad. A number of producers I talked to regularly book guests from this publication. Subtract the cost of postage, printing, and phone calls, and, if you can afford it, consider whether your royalties on this or your *next* book will pay for this privilege. Do it if you can.

12
TV Jeebies.

Getting TV exposure for your book takes luck. And hard work. And hard work. And hard work. And hard work. And luck, luck, luck.

If your luck is running very strong, you will get a feature story in a major newspaper, and the TV stations will call you. Sometimes it does happen that way. More often than not, it won't. You really have to work for what you get with TV. You have to be more persistent than with any other medium.

Unlike talk radio, which is searching for interesting people willing to talk about interesting things, TV is choosing from the entire universe of subjects, and isn't quite so needy. Still, just because the odds are higher doesn't mean that you don't want to tackle them. You just have to bait a lot more hooks, and you have to expect that, while you may be successful less often, when you do score, you score with more impact than with print or radio.

There are only three or four kinds of local TV shows on which the novice has the opportunity to appear. They are news programs, news shows which have an associated live talk segment, local morning shows, and newsmagazines. The News/Noise principles apply here, only more so. The better the news angle, or the louder the noise, the better your odds of getting TV time.

Making The Evening News

If you have written something that is relevant to an immediately breaking or ongoing news story, don't even bother reading the rest of this book until you have put a telephone in your hand. Call the most popular TV station right now (they're all listed in your phone book), and ask the receptionist for the news desk. She'll put you through. Ask for the name of the news producer and if s/he is available. If you get a stall or a "...not available right now. Can s/he call you back?" use your most succinct style to explain that you are *the author* of *Don't Swallow That!*, and that you have something relevant to add to the story about the baby in the drain pipe with the open safety pin in her throat. (Or whatever is appropriate to your book and their story.) If you don't get through to the producer and/or get an immediate positive response, leave your telephone number(s), tell the person on the phone that you will be contacting other TV stations, but that they are your first choice, so you will try to stay available. Thank her or him politely for the help, *and call the next most popular TV station* until you do get a positive response. If you get to the bottom of the list without a positive response, call the stations again from the top. If you still don't get any response, you may want to review your presentation of your credentials for the next time. Go on to the radio talk shows.

Now, let's suppose they do call you back. TV news shows often like to fill stories with interviews with "experts." It gives the camera something to break away to, and fills in a wider picture for viewers. If you are called back by a TV news producer, she or he may make arrangements with you to have a camera crew show up at your office to film your comments for inclusion in the evening broadcast. Or you may work out a good, visually interesting location such as your back porch or a nearby parking lot. A location appropriate to the story. Or the producer may ask you to come into the studio to do a live or taped commentary.

Put on your most business-like clothing, especially if you are going to be talking about a serious subject. Even if your book is called *Be A Clown!* and you're discussing some scandal with the elephant trainer, dressing up in greasepaint and green hair will not make you look more like you know what you're talking about. It will, most likely, only make you look foolish. Likewise, when you're on camera, *don't even try to work in the name of your book.* It sounds tacky, and self-serving on a news show. (Not that you don't want to serve the best interest of your book, it's just that TV is a medium of quick impressions, and you want to make the best one possible.) The host will usually include the name of the book you've written in your introduction, because it's the credential (or one of the credentials) that got you on the show in the first place. If you're not particularly well known in your community, then the station will also usually run a "super" (superimposed text on a picture) at the bottom of the screen with your name and "Author of *Licking Buff Toads: A New Low In Getting High.*"

TV is not only immediate, it's abbreviated. There is never enough time for complicated analysis or detailed explanation. If you have demonstration props—a plastic, exposed alimentary canal, a break-away tooth socket, or something that will *simplify* your explanation—bring it. Also bring charts or graphs, but *only, only, only* if they simplify the current situation. Offer them to the producer and let the producer make the decision about whether to use them. (Don't surprise a producer. They hate that.) The more simplistic, clear, and understandable you can make your explanation of a situation, the more valuable you become to TV news. And the more likely the producer will be to call you back to "expert" other stories.

You're The Expert

You may not get an immediate response from any TV news shows. Of course, go on to the radio shows to see what you can drum up, but don't give up on TV. In your initial contact with any news producers who have made a decision not to use your services, don't make them feel guilty. It doesn't work. Just offer to send a copy of the book and to be available should they need you on this or any other related story. (Remember, producers of all flavors could care less about promoting your book. What they care passionately about is getting a good and interesting show.) If you can establish yourself with the producer as the expert-of-record in a given field, you stand a better chance of getting on the air. Send the book right away, with *two* business cards (one stapled to the inside cover of the book) and a *brief* note reminding her/him of your relevance to a particular story and your expertise in a particular area or areas. If you have a computer that can manufacturer rolodex cards, make up several with your name and phone number, *each headed with a different aspect of your area of expertise* (i.e.: Garden Studies, Roses, Pesticides), and include the set of them with your business card. (If you're sending rolodex cards, just send one business card.)

If you don't have a strong connection to a current news story, keep watching. When anything happens that makes you relevant, get on the phone immediately. These opportunities do not come along often, and they evaporate even faster. If you miss them, they're gone.

There's also nothing to stop you from sending a couple of copies of your book, *Men Who Keep Pets And The Women Who Pay For The*

Purina, to the news producers *in advance of any story*. Send the same packet, and in your letter offer to be an on-air commentator should your subject come up.

If you want to save books, just send a letter, a business card, and a set of rolodex cards. Then when they need someone to talk about the historic uses of shaving cream, or how oranges increase your sex drive, or whatever it is that you know all about, there's a chance they'll call you.

You can also *call the station with a story idea*. Ask for the news room assignment desk, and say that you have a story about _____, "does that match up with what any of your producers is working on?" If they say, "No" then ask which producer normally handles that kind of story. Get a name. Get a name. Get a name. Then get that name on the phone and go to work.

And by all means, if you have *ever* done this before, or ever had any time on camera, be absolutely sure you mention this. The last thing that a producer wants to do is look like a fool for booking someone who freezes when the red light on the camera goes on. If you haven't been on camera before, go borrow or rent a video cam, and with a good, supportive friend, set yourself up in a chair, and start practicing. Keep practicing in front of the camera till you can stop cringing when you look at the playback. Then you can honestly tell the producer that you "have no trouble being on camera." (Don't, however, tell him/her that you know this because you've rehearsed at home on your rented Magnavox.)

Local morning TV talk shows and talk shows connected with the "news *at this hour*" (as opposed to what?) are handled much the same as national talk shows, only the scale is smaller, the intensity is somewhat lower, and the calls aren't as expensive. (They also don't put you up in a nice hotel.) Take your cues from the next chapter and reduce the local talk shows to the appropriate scale.

Make The Producer's Life Easier

The key to the local video magazines is the producers. To find them, either pick up your telephone book, call the station and ask, or pop a tape into your VCR and punch the record button for the show you want to be on. At the end of the program, you'll find the "crawl" which is the list of credits of people involved in the show that crawl up the screen (sometimes very rapidly). They often include the names of the executive producer, producer, and sometimes segment producers. These are the names you want to add to your resource database. These are the people you want to pursue—as you have pursued everything else—with the best show or segment angle you can come up with and a plan to make their jobs easier.

Suggest other guests, particularly ones you can supply. And, of course, since TV is a visual medium, *be prepared with interesting suggestions for a filming location.* The first time I did a local newsmagazine, I invited them, with my own producer's approval, to film during my radio show. The second time, I invited the camera into my house, and then I filled it with interesting people who were willing to simulate a parents' support group.

What You Need To Know On The Air.

There are three things to keep in mind when you do this kind of a show. 1) You will never be thrilled with the way you look. 2) Something brilliant you said will get cut or edited into a strange context. And 3) unless you're the cover story of the newsmagazine or the only talk show guest for the segment, your fifteen minutes of fame may be something more like five or less. If you do make the cover story, you may get as much as *eight* whole minutes of television time plus bumpers and teasers (those little snippets before commercials and other segments designed to keep people from switching to "Let's Make A Deal" reruns).

What you can do about:

1) **appearance**:

News shows and locals almost never have hair or makeup people available. If you're concerned, call your local beauty salon or school, or college or university's production department and ask to talk to someone who knows about TV makeup. TV makeup is different than regular makeup, so even women who know Max Factor from Maxwell Smart may not be all that smart about what makes them look good under bad lights. For the men...well...remember what General Noriega looked like on the news without any makeup and decide for yourself if you want some.

Some no-no's about dressing. I always try to wear something I've worn before. First, because I want to be in something that I feel comfortable moving in, and that I have worn in front of people before, so I know its effect. And secondly, because those nasty price, cleaning, and inspection tags have a sneaky habit of not always getting themselves removed when you're under pressure, so I could look genuinely silly to hundreds of thousands of people all at once if I miss one and raise my arm to make a point, or the camera person decides to shoot up my nose from my knees in an "artistic" angle and the tag shows up. This is as true for men's clothes as it is for women's.

Bright, solid red is always a bad choice because there is never any control over how people at home have the color on their sets adjusted. Red often tends to "blossom" or "bloom" (a kind of uncontrolled brilliant ghost color). It even has its own negative term, "broadcast red," to describe its ill effects. So even if you wrote *Aura's Are All Around You*, chose another color.

Another item to leave hanging in your closet is anything with narrow stripes or glen plaid. That causes a "moiré" (more-ay) pattern, which is that sort of traveling wavy line that can make everyone a little nauseous and throw the audience into seizures. You've seen it in the suits of game show contestants and other newcomers to the screen. Opt for a nice, sincere, patternless, medium-blue instead.

2) **bad editing**:

Keep your comments brief. Not the *overall* time (you want to get in as much as you possibly can in a natural tone and at a natural pace), but *the sentences*. Keep those short. Your comments will *always* be more than they can use, and they will *always* be edited. So if you have long, complicated sentences, you make the editor want to tear out hair (probably yours), you make it difficult to edit your piece, and some vital part of your thought necessarily gets left behind. The shorter sentences are really your best chance of having what you mean match what they show on TV. They may seem choppy to you at first. If you can't do it now, practice.

3) **so much you, so little time**:

Practice being pithy. Know your book's salient points, and then, most importantly, don't share all of them. Don't give away the store. *Figure out what's intriguing about what you wrote, what's amusing or entertaining, or will make viewers want to know more, and talk briefly from those points.* Also, it really helps if you have a good idea beforehand of some of the specific things you want to say, so you don't stumble in front of the camera. It's not that producers are particularly meaner than any other slice of humanity. It's just that they have an enormous amount of power over how you look in front of potential fans and you don't want to temp them into breaching the privilege of knowing you by showing you stuttering, stammering, or spitting on the camera operator. Producers thrive on controversy. That's not the kind you want to give them.

Keep a book in sight. In your hands, on the coffee table, on the desk in front of you. Pick it up. Leaf through it as though you are looking for something. Ask the producer if s/he would like a cover shot "here, or will s/he get it in the studio?" You can say things like, "In my book, (hold up or nod toward book) *There's No Good News On TV*, I say..." or "When I wrote *Julius Caesar Was A Commie*, I found out that..." This isn't TV news. You have the latitude to push harder.

A note to fiction writers: since it's harder to get TV coverage for fiction, you can often get the attention of the local nightly newsmagazine with something you create or put together. How about a fascinating panel of three women, one of whom wrote a mystery novel, a criminal defense attorney, and a woman who served time for murder? Find them a topic in common, and you could get a few video minutes. Do you know two articulate people who wrote government exposes? Could you convince them to come on TV? Could you, the author of *Who Pruned The Wallflower?*, put together a party expert, and one or two survivors of terrible parties? For fiction writers, the possibilities are only limited by your imagination, and your rolodex. Fiction publicity is almost always a matter of noise, not news. Come up with your own ideas of what groups might make interesting TV and use that to give you and your book some exposure.

TV References

Bacon's Radio/TV Directory
This is the companion to Beacon's Publicity Checker for print. Not all libraries carry it either, so you may still have to call a friend in an advertising or PR agency to find it. You can also buy it. A year's subscription costs $150 + $5. Call 1(800) 621-0561

Broadcast & Cable Yearbook

Directories in Print-Broadcast Media Section
Charles B. Montney, Editor

Gale Directory of Publications and Broadcast Media
Karen Troskynski Thomas & Deborah M. Burk, Editors

If you have a little more money, and you want to do a little less work, here is another option:

TV-Radio Interview Reports   Phone: 1(800) 989-1400, ext. 703
Bradley Communications Corp., P.O. Box 1206, Landsdowne, PA 19050
A bimonthly "magazine" of 1/4-, 1/2-, and full-page display ads sent to 4,000 radio and TV producers in the United States. A single 1/2-page ad run in 1 issue will cost you $325, and an average expenditure is from $600 to $900. All they need is a copy of your book, a photo, and your check, and they'll write your ad. A number of producers I talked to regularly book guests from this book. Although there are no guarantees, you should measure the cost against selling thirty- to fifty-thousand books from national TV appearances. Plus, of course, you get exposure to radio producers as well. If you can afford it, this is a real investment in your own work. If you can't afford it, see if your publisher will spring for the cost. Or redeem soda cans till you save up enough. Being in there could save you years of work.

13
Talk Fast. You Have Fifteen Seconds.

Oprah. Phil. Sally. Geraldo. Montel. Bertrice. Jane. Joan. Rikki. Jerry. And that's just the talk in the middle of the day. At night there's Jay, David, Arsenio, and who ever replaces the Pat/Chevy/Dennis wannabees on the other channels. For a book writer seeking publicity, this is the big time. It is said that an appearance on one of these shows can move *fifty thousand* books.

If you think that the competition by book writers is tough for regular TV, you can only begin to imagine how many are already in line for an appearance amidst all the dysfunctionals, the bizarros, the politicos, the show offs, and the just plain publicity hungry.

To get booked on one of these, it helps to have won the National Book Award and the Pulitzer. It helps even more to be Cher's sister. Or to reveal Cher's bedroom or makeup secrets. And that only puts you in line behind Barbra or Sly or all the president's men and women whenever they choose to raise their hands.

But, on the presumption that nothing's impossible, here's how to go about getting booked.

"*If* you can get me on the phone, you have exactly *fifteen seconds* to catch my interest," said one TV talk show producer who was a guest on another talk show. "I'm always on deadline," she said. "I have people screaming at me from every corner. Three people standing over my desk breathing down my neck. Don't get me wrong, I need show ideas. But I don't need any schmoozing. Get to the point. Get my attention. And get on with it. I may not book the caller that minute, but if they can get my attention, I'll take a phone number and get back to them when I can either work them into a show, or can get the show they suggested sold at a story conference."

Well, there you have it. Now you know exactly what to do once you have the producer of a major talk show on the phone. You've already learned how to do a one-minute pitch. With these folks, that's too long. To make it in the Big Time you have to talk faster.

What's that, you say? How do you actually get a producer of one of those shows on the phone? You ask for them by name. To get those names, you use every source you can find and anything else you can think up. Does it really make a difference? Especially if you have a swell idea or a great book to begin with? You betcha!

The difference of not having a name versus having a name was dramatically demonstrated to me when I first tried to contact the people at Harpo (Oprah spelled backwards) Productions. My files have two very different responses to nearly exactly the same package. The first, including a book and a videotape clip of a previous newsmagazine appearance, was sent with an open-ended letter addressed to the Executive Producer. The first submission netted me an unsigned form rejection reply dismissing my "show idea" as politely as a form letter could. Since, at that point, I didn't know that it was even a good idea to submit a *show idea*, I wondered how my package ended up in the wrong stack for replies—obviously the one for wretches who wanted to talk about having their legs waxed by their stepfathers.

Befriending a number of independent producers and camera people, I figured out that they might have access to insider's lists I didn't, and that they might be willing to share. They were, and another letter was dispatched, this time with a personal note to a specific person by name. It was nearly the identical package, but this time I got a much more positive reaction.

And...I have a little surprise for you. I'm willing to share too. I can't give you the names of the producers of the big talk shows, because they change too often. But the least I can do is give you the shows' addresses and/or phone numbers. You can find out the names for yourself with a pencil, a piece of paper, and a VCR. Just tape the shows you are interested in, or the ones you think would be interested in you. At the end, look at the credit crawl. Just like you did to get the producer's name for the local newsmagazine. In this case, there should be several of them. Choose one, and make contact. Incidentally, this is one of those places where you really shouldn't be speaking for yourself if you can help it. Get your most articulate, coolest, most phone-savvy, and PR-savvy friend to make the call for you, *as your publicist*. Just make sure that s/he knows how much the first seconds count. Worst case, become your own publicist. Substitute a Nom de Guerre that doesn't sound like a fake version of your own name. Am I suggesting that you aren't entirely truthful about your identity just to make a connection with the producer? My answer has to be "*fifty thousand books!*" Decide for yourself what is a morality problem for you and act accordingly.

LESS IS BETTER! Write tight.

Whether you get immediate interest or not, send in a follow-up package. This should include:

- a *very brief* letter acknowledging your phone conversation
- a copy of your book
- a couple of impressive reviews
- a synopsis/fact sheet of your show idea in a bulleted format (for quick and easy reference)

- a list of credits and previous guest appearances (to reassure the producer that you won't freeze up on the set)
- a business card and/or a rolodex card headed with your area of expertise, your name, and phone number

Do not trust your precious package to the U.S. Postal Service. Send it by one of the overnight or second-day freight shippers like Fedex, Airborne, or UPS. After you've sent your package in, *give it a full week* before you call back. Then don't just ask if they got your stuff. Say that you are calling to give them one new idea or brilliant thought. Don't leave this to chance. Figure out something impressive that you can leave out of your package without damage, and be prepared to pitch it on the follow-up call.

Learn From Your Rejections.

If a producer doesn't express any interest, ask "What is it about my book that doesn't interest you?" See if the answer gives you an insight into how to approach the next producer. If your book is too close to a subject that has recently been done, ask, "When do you think would be a good time to get back to the issue?" When you get that answer, let the producer know that you'll call back. "Can I call you back in April when my new book on a similar subject comes out?" (Even if you *don't* have a new book coming out. By April the producer probably won't remember.) Put a reminder in your day/dater to dial again. By then you will have sold x thousand more books, made a bestseller list somewhere, and/or made some news or noise you can talk about to make you seem an even more desirable show guest.

...Heeeeeeeere's You.

Hooray, they're going to book you! What do you need to know?

- Yes, most of the time the show will fly you in
- Yes, they will put you up in a nice hotel with room service.
- Maybe, they'll send a car to pick you up.
- Probably they will have a person available who does hair and makeup. You should ask the producer about this when s/he is making the other arrangements
- Yes, there is a Green Room where you will be waiting with the other guests on the show.

Before you go on, if you are walking onto the set from offstage, you will be fitted with a small, wireless lavaliere microphone affixed to your shirt or blouse, or a wired mike will be waiting at your seat. This has a spring clip that you should attach at about collarbone level. Remember not to strike your chest, or adjust your clothing in a way that makes the mike rub against cloth.

Relax as best you can. You only have two choices when the red light goes on. You can make a fool of yourself, or not. Choose not. Remember, you're a pro, and you do have interesting things to say. Things you've already said in your book. Things you've talked about repeatedly on other shows. And in your own living room. You'll be fabulous.

One or two more things on where and how you look on camera. First, where: *Don't look directly toward the camera. Don't talk directly into the lens.* Talk to the host or any questioner in the audience, and let the camera find you. You're not as practiced at being on TV as, oh, for example, a pro news anchor, so, for you, following the bouncing red camera light can be confusing. Also, it's very disconcerting for the audience to be confronted with the intimacy of electronic eye-contact when all it expected to do was eavesdrop on a conversation between you and the host.

Now a word about *how* you look. When you are talking on camera, *hold your head still.* This will take some practice and concentration to master, but it is what professionals do. If you run a video tape of TV amateurs on fast forward, you'll see heads bobbing and weaving so much that you may need seasick medication to calm the queasiness. Now tape a portion of the evening news, any evening news, and watch the pros. Heads stay still and poised elegantly over necks, where they are supposed to be. Even at fast forward, they hardly vary position. There's a reason for that. In radio the natural, conversational head bobbing throws your voice off-mike, which makes you hard to listen to. That's not the problem on TV. On TV, your mike travels with your body. The problem is that you can end up looking like a puppet on speed. The best cure I've heard is to imagine that you have a copy of your book balanced on your head (several if your book is very light), and walk, talk, and sit accordingly. If nothing else, worrying about imaginary slippage will take your mind off the fact that several million people are watching your every move.

Now, knowing all that, you can relax. You're going to be great!

You Owe Me One For These

Show	Address	Phone
Phil Donahue	30 Rockefeller Plaza NY, NY 10112	(212) 664-6501
Maury Povitch	221 W. 26th St. NY, NY 10001	(212) 989-3622
Sally Jesse Raphael	75 Rockefeller Plaza NY, NY 10011	(212)332-2000
Geraldo Rivera	Investigative News Group CBS Broadcast Center	

Joan Rivers	51 W. 52nd St NY, NY 10021 524 W. 57th Street NY, NY 10019	
Jerry Springer	454 N. Columbus Dr. Chicago. Ill 66011	(312) 321-5350
Today Show	30 Rockefeller Plaza NY, NY 10112	(212) 664-4249
Tonight Show	3000 W. Alameda Ave Burbank, CA 91543	(818) 840-2222
Montel Williams	1500 Broadway, Ste 700 NY, NY 10036	
Oprah Winfrey	Harpo Productions 110 Carpenter St. Chicago, Ill 60607	(312) 633-1000

14
Okay, Okay, Do A Press Release.

It's an absolute staple of the publicity business, and, as far as I'm concerned, about as interesting as old Keds. The thing about press releases is that everybody does them. And hardly anybody reads them.

There are scores of PR professionals who would defend to their last paycheck the press release's efficacy and efficiency. I'm really of a mixed mind. I have seen specialty magazines run press releases practically verbatim because they needed filler. I have seen press releases waste-basketed on discovery. More often the later than the former.

Here's when I recommend sending a press release: 1) When you've exhausted all the more immediate publicity-generating efforts. 2) When you don't have a lot to say. 3) When you want to send backup information to reinforce efforts you've already made. 4) When you want to keep your name in front of resources who have already said, "No." And 5) while you're working up your courage to tackle the media more directly.

As you can tell, I consider press releases a secondary effort that usually can't do any harm, and occasionally can actually do some good. I especially like them when someone else is picking up the postage. Which brings me to the best time to send out a press release on your book: any time your publisher is doing a general mailing to either bookstores or the press *for any other reason.* (Something you are only likely to know if your publisher is a small one.) Then a press release should go out on your publisher's stationery. It's a free and available opportunity to get your name and your book's name in front of an important audience one more time. If you provide the written release, many publishers will be happy to do the copying and include it in their envelope. How could that hurt?

At the very least, the recipient will glance at the headline before tossing it in the round file, so you've got that one opportunity to make an impression. If you use the News/Noise principles we've outlined so far to create that headline, you may stand a somewhat better chance of having the body of the release actually read. For example:

`Author Contends Extraterrestrial Elected Veep in '88.`

Just in case you've never written a press release before, or don't know anyone whom you can arm-twist into doing it for you, here's how to write one:

- Start with a letterhead, if you have one. Even better, use someone else's. If the publisher won't post your press release on its own letterhead, and you either can't afford a PR agent or can't talk your friend who does this for a living into doing this for you on her office stationery, then here are some other options.

- Create an imaginative, imaginary company name and letterhead on your computer. (*The Absolutely Greatest PR Company On The Planet, Inc.*; *Publicity R Us*; *The Loud Team*; *VandenGraph, Vandenheuval, & Bluementhal PR Esq.*; whatever.) If you plan to continue using this company name in any way that generates income, as opposed to being a ghost company for sending out PR material, be sure to check your state's prerequisites for fictitious company names, and doing-business-as requirements such as licenses, fees, and exams first.

- Use an out of town address. Have your cousin rent a cheap post office box in some other city, to give an address different from yours. Or just rent one of your own, across town. That way you don't have to give out your own, and, again, nobody really knows you're doing this yourself. Dealing with third parties in this publicity business keeps the egos at a distance. Rather than having to deal with an amateur or risk hurting your feelings, people with booking power prefer to negotiate with someone other than you.

A standard release, for reasons far beyond my comprehension, should look as if it was typed on a 1946 Smith Corona typewriter, (even if you have an IBM 20986 Incredula Super-Modula computer with six chained gigabyte hard drives in your den/guest room/ tax-deductible home office). So that means you use a Courier or a Prestige Elite typeface (or one that looks typewriterish) in a 10 or 12 point size. Don't ask me why, I don't know. Just because it's done that way. Later we'll talk about deviating. For now, this is how it's done by the pros. Here's the boring stuff:

- The release is double spaced with one-inch margins on each side and a three-quarter inch bottom margin. (The top depends on whether you have a letterhead or not.) There is no greeting. At the upper right hand side, below the letter head, should be the following:

          FOR IMMEDIATE RELEASE
          CONTACT Minerva J. Mouse
                    (312) 555-9190

(...What if they call that number, it's yours, and *you* answer? Break out the champagne. They called. They want you. They got you. Charade's over. Schedule something.)

- Use your spouse's name, your mother's name, your kid's name, your cousin's name, or your best friend's name as contact. (With their permission, please.) As long as their last name is different from yours.

- The headline follows the contact information, and is usually in the same boring typewriter font as the letter body, though often times it is underlined, to set it apart. Keep it short, (under 10 words) punchy, and capture the essence of the most newsworthy aspect of your book.

Government Rats Cause Cancer In Canadian Laboratory Workers

- The body of the press release tells the rest of the news/noise story. But it isn't a news story, so it doesn't have to stay objective. It could rave about your reviews. It could explain how you bring a brilliant, new perspective, a Hemingway-esque writing style to an old genre, or have won the first Pulitzer ever awarded for a book written while the author stood on his/her head. Because we are of a herd mentality, we all want to be where the rest of us are going. So your release should tout the excitement of the crowd. Did more people show up for your book signing than went to the K-Mart opening? Use a lot of exclamation points!!! Yet another printing? The higher the number, the more exclamation points in the headline: ...*FIFTH printing!!!!!*

- Normally the body is no more than two pages. If you do go to a second page, print it on the back side, and at the bottom of the first page put:

          - more -

It'll really make 'em think you know what you're doing. (Or that your cousin/publicist does.) If you're hoping for interviews, make the last couple of lines biographical. "X lives in East Armchair, MS, with her rich uncle and 27 cats." Whatever tidbits make you seem interviewable. Then give them your phone number again: "For an interview, call (312) 555-9190." Yes, it is the same one on the contact line on the top of the release.

* And finally—Standard Press Releases all end the same way:

- 30 -

The very idea that there is a standard makes me immediately want to break the standard. When I do a press release, I keep just enough of the format to let any fool who cares if I am doing it *right* happy. I keep the letterhead, the FOR IMMEDIATE RELEASE and contact lines, the -more-, and -30- designations. Then I get cookin'. I fool with the typefaces to make it interesting. I scan a picture onto the page. I sign it in simulated blood. I do whatever it takes **TO GET SOMEBODY'S ATTENTION!!!**

So should you.

- 30 -

15
Hug Your Bookstore.

That's pretty much it for the media. But that's not the only place you need to take care of business. While it's true that you are in the book *creating* and the book *promoting* business, and not in the book *selling* business, without bookstores, you're out of business. Bookstores can mean the difference between having to ask people if they "want that with fries" for a living, or hanging out at your beach house by the pool while the butler fends off the press. Well, okay, maybe it really only means that you get to write another book, and another, and another till you can afford to make an offer on the house with the butler and the pool.

Bookstores are a critical part of the process.

If book buyers don't know you or your work, the worst thing they can do is not order your book.

The next worst thing they can do is to order some. Just a few. Then put them on the shelf spine out, and leave them to fend for themselves. In that store, unless you've got your media cranking, consider yourself history. In order to return unsold books to a distributor, the bookstore has to pay the freight *both ways*, plus a hefty five- to fifteen-percent penalty for the mistake of ordering a book that didn't move. Yours. So it shouldn't be any surprise to you that bookstores order only a fraction of what they're offered. Or that they reorder authors who have sold well for them in the past. Book buyers generally stay with what they know. After all, it's their jobs, their reputations, sometimes even their businesses on the line.

But get book buyers interested in you, and they buy you and put your book face out on the shelf, or in a nifty little pile by the cash register. They also buy books they have a good feeling about, think will sell well, or know has a spitload of publicity coming in. If you do make Oprah or Phil, get out a special mailing to the bookstores. Better yet, have your publisher do it. Bookstores will need to know with enough time to get deliveries and give you the front window display.

What else can a bookstore do for you? Mine threw me a birthday party. The owner found out that my b-day coincided with my pub date, and conspired with my best friend. They invited three or four thousand of my other best friends and their closest potential customers. Of course, not all of them showed up. But every last one of them got an invitation with my name and the name of the book on it. Next time they're in any bookstore, it'll be hard to resist at least picking up the book to find out what all the fuss was about. In one day, the bookstore owner sold what would have taken three months without the event. Plus, he got a lot of new people into the store at a critical Christmas buying time. And I got to dress up and sign autographs. So a good time was had by all.

Don't expect your bookstore to throw you a bash. But they can give you some more conventional consideration. If they know that you live nearby, usually they will order your book so you have a place to send buyers. Most of them like being the "pet bookstore" of a local author. In fact, there are a lot of things a bookstore can do—how about a window full of your books? Or an end-aisle display?—once they know that you work to promote your book so that it moves off their shelves.

Stop In And Drop Off

Whether you're in your home city, or out of state, it never hurts to stop by every bookstore you encounter with your boast book. Tell the clerk at the register that you're an author, and watch a couple of eyes light up. (Bookstore clerks love writers.) Not all that many authors bother to stop in and shake hands. Ask at the register where you can find the book buyer. Then go introduce yourself and your book.

Does it really make any difference? It does according to one book buyer I met when I happened to be driving through Raleigh, North Carolina. She thanked me for stopping in, and said she'd seen my book in one of the catalogs that crossed her desk. But with so many publishing company's catalogs coming in, she explained that there was no way to tell which were the we'll-be-really-sorry-if-we-under-order's and which were the ho-hum's. So a side trip of maybe fifteen or twenty miles out of my way let her make a decision to buy. "Sure," you're probably saying, "a couple of books here, a tiny order there, what's the deal?" Well, as it turned out, she was the buyer for three fairly good sized stores in a mini-chain. When next year's catalog crosses her desk, she'll be looking for my newest. Just because I went out of my way to shake hands.

Many authors I talked to feel funny about hawking their books directly to the stores. They feel that it's demeaning. I promise you that I will feel exactly the same way just as soon as one or two of mine makes the *New York Times* bestseller list. Till then, I'll put up with the embarrassment. Even during those times when I just can't put it out there, I try to do it anyway. I walk into a bookstore because it's where the payoff is.

Just go in and check the shelves to see if your book is in stock. If it is, ask to see the store manager, owner, or buyer and introduce yourself. Say that you "just stopped in to sign their stock." (Remember how signed books sell better? That's the part that's good for the bookstore. The part that's good for you is that signed books often get placed at the cash register, or in a featured section, *and they sell better*.) If they don't have the book in stock, or you can't get to the shelves to check before you're turned over to the buyer or owner, just say that you wanted to introduce yourself, sign any books they have in stock, or offer them a seed order (three to five books) of signed books. No one's going to throw you out of the store. Even if they don't buy.

Talk with your publisher about how invoicing should be handled when you do this. Sometimes, with tiny bookstores or independents, collecting on these orders can be more of a nuisance than it's worth. Some publishers will ask you not to place more than three books to lower their risk. Some will want you to get a check made out to the publisher on the spot, which is usually impossible and sometimes rude when you are asking a buyer for the favor of taking your book. Some publishers will want copies of the invoices faxed to them immediately upon sale so they can put the store into a collection and follow-up file. And some publishers don't want you to place *any* orders yourself because it messes up their inventory and invoicing system. In that case, just stop by the bookstore with a show-and-tell copy of the book, and your PR kit. Tell them who's distributing, and let the book buyer copy the *ISBN number*, the number above the set of barcode lines usually on the back cover, for ordering.

I also made up small, round pressure sensitive stickers that say, "*Signed Copy*" on my computer, at the suggestion of a bookstore owner in Boston.

It turned out to be a great idea. Most, but not all larger bookstores have their own. Smaller bookstores usually don't and are delighted. They want whatever will help them sell books. It's an easy task to do on your home computer. Don't just automatically apply the stickers before you deliver the books. Some stores have collector customers who think that stickers make the tome less valuable, and prefer just a signature.

The hard and fast rule about what to do for bookstores is this: *Do whatever they'd like that will help them sell your book, and not a whit more.* While some stores appreciate posters and novelties that you can generate on your computer, some don't have the wall space, the counter space, or the time to do displays. Some don't want to be bothered. Some will just soak up whatever you can give them. Always ask first. Bookstore people will usually be happy to tell you. And thrilled that you asked.

Here's one thing you can do even if you don't introduce yourself, and that you don't *ever* ask about: you can *"face your book."* This means inconspicuously walking up to the shelf your book is on, and turning it *so the cover faces out.* It gives the book a better, more eye-catching display. Chances are it will stay that way, at least for a while. And I don't know an author who hasn't done it.

Sign Here.

Then there are book signings.

You'll want to set up as many of these as you can. They are good practice for meeting your public, and letting bookstores get to know you. They are also not difficult to arrange, unless you live in New York City, where they will always set up signings for Ivana Trump, and less often set them up for lesser known lights.

Ask your publisher for a list of bookstores in your region. For the stores within easy driving distance, drive over. Introduce yourself the same way I've already suggested, and if the buyer indicates that s/he will be doing some ordering, ask if the store would like to have you do a signing. You'll get an immediate answer. If that answer is "No," smile and go on to the next bookstore. Real live authors are still a relative rarity in bookstores. Someone somewhere will say "Yes."

For bookstores within a two or three hundred mile driving radius, use the phone. (Yes, of course you could send a personal note if you know a name. But it's slower, and requires that someone take the time to reply. I'd rather call.) Ask for the bookstore owner, not the buyer. If the owner can't or doesn't schedule the signings, s/he will pass you on to the proper person. Be respectful—you're asking for a favor, not granting one. Introduce yourself as the author of *Was Doctor Scholl A Foot Fetishist?*, published by XYZ publishing and distributed by Such and Such Distributor. Then say what you want. It could be that you will be in the area on specific dates and that you are setting up signings and you "certainly wouldn't want to leave this store out." Or it could just be a simple inquiry as to whether they'd be interested in setting up a signing, and when would be the most convenient?

For bookstores beyond that radius it gets more difficult. It's hard to imagine the advantage of driving eight hours just to sign a couple of dozen copies. Or justifying the airplane expenses. But, on the other hand, if you are going out of town on other business, or to celebrate your sister's fifth wedding, *and you know at least two months in advance*, then it is possible, and even advisable to see what you can set up. If phone numbers aren't included on the publishers list, then head for the library. This time to the phone directory section, and copy every bookstore's name and number in the destination city. Start with the biggest stores likely to be carrying or wanting to carry your book. After your introduction, let them know exactly when you would be available. Day, date, and time. If they bite, they will want to have enough time to do some publicity on your behalf. Any less time, and they will have missed important local monthly calendar closings, or won't have enough advance warning to rev up their ad department. Just keep going down the list until you have all your spare time filled with signings. For every store that declines a signing, let them know that you will be stopping by to say hello and sign any stock they have on hand. But only if your schedule allows you to actually show up. No point in making enemies if you can't make it.

Now on to the actual mechanics of book signings. Some bookstores want to make a big deal of them. They set a schedule, place ads in the paper, brew a vat of coffee, and get out the petit fours. Others will just put a handwritten sign up on the door or near the cash register, and some will invite you and not bother to tell anyone you're coming. Some prefer that you just sign the copies they have on hand, and not make a big deal about it.

Book signings are a lesson in humility. They are also very good for business. When you talk to the manager or owner about doing one, be sure to mention any media appearances you'll be making. Then ask what the store usually does, if anything, to publicize their signings. Don't let them get away with saying, "Aw, nothing much." Find out how much nothing. Then do some more yourself. If they're running ads, get them a good photo or a book cover for the ad. Mention the when and where of the signing on any local radio or TV shows. Be helpful. You're helping yourself. And the more publicity your signing gets, the more books you'll sell.

By the way, about the signing itself: *Don't expect anyone to actually show up.* What? Nobody?!!! Right. It's an everyday occurrence for book signings.

Or, if some people actually do show up, they might just stand around the corner, behind a pillar, or in the other room. They may come up and say the most absurd, surprising, tongue-tied things. Most readers like the anonymous intimacy that reading gives them one-to-one with the author. But that's really different from walking up and starting a cogent conversation with a real, live celebrity who wrote a book. Don't take it personally. Or even as an indication of the quality of your book. There is some law of nature governing book signings that reverses all that your experience interacting with people has taught you. Book signings are intimidating to buyers.

When it happens to you, just reassure the book person who has been assigned to sit with you, slip books under your pen, and make you feel like Your Exhaulted Authorship, that it's all right, that you know that signings are often like that, and that you know that the signed books you leave behind will probably all be gone within the week. It'll make your "assistant" think you are one cool dude or dudette. This probably doesn't happen to Howard Stern or Barbara Cartland. But, more than likely, it will happen to you until you've sold as many copies of anything as they have. And the books probably *will* be gone within the week. Or at least the month. Signed books have a value all their own. The plain fact is that people value signed books, but it's somehow easier on them to come by the store after you've gone home.

How many people show up at a book signing is in direct proportion to how much publicity has been generated about your appearance and how brave your readers are.

While many don't, some stores require a reading with the signing. Ask how much time is usually devoted to doing the reading, and pick your selection accordingly. Choose passages that show off your style, that tantalize with content, but that don't give away the plot or share the secret surprise. Remember, your purpose is to entice listeners into buying or recommending from what they heard. Choose the most delicious parts, but always serve them up an appetizer, never the full course.

16
The Practical Art Of Cross-Ruffing.

Everything...absolutely everything builds on everything else.

It doesn't matter what comes first or second. The second you get something working on behalf of your book, you should be using it to get more and more publicity.

Some of that will take care of itself. When a major newspaper runs a story on you, you will probably get calls from the producers of the local talk shows. The local, independent TV station or TV newsmagazine may also call to set up shooting a segment. Rarely will print come after you because of broadcast media exposure. (Another fact of the known universe for an unknown reason.) To assist this process, *be sure to tell the reporter or editor that it is all right to give your phone number to any other inquiring media.*

You should use everything you can and everything you already have to get whatever else you can arrange.

Your reviews should go into your boast book. So should a list of the shows you've appeared on.

When you're writing to or calling radio producers, let them know that you've done this before. Include a short list of where.

If a station asked you back or said something especially nice about you as a guest, ask them to write you a note to that effect. Let them know that you will be using a copy of their letter to send to other stations. Most will be happy to do it for you. Many will ask you to write the letter, and they will have it rewritten on their stationery, signed, and sent or faxed back to you.

If you are featured on a local TV station, get copies of the segment. Ask the producer for a 3/4-inch copy as well as a VHS copy. The 3/4-inch tape is the professional size that will not play in your home VCR, but will edit better if you use a professional studio (which I recommend you do). The 3/4-inch gives a higher grade picture, and won't lose so much quality when you make copies. My hometown has a couple of easy, accessible video editing facilities. So should yours. They may be called Video Edit, Video Town, or Quick Video or something similar. There is a per-hour cost for editing, a different cost if you use one of their editors, and a per-cassette charge for making copies or "dubs." It's a good investment as I already suggested in the section on getting onto the talk shows.

If you really don't have the budget for professional assistance, then use two home VCR's to make copies of your segments, and include them in whatever packets you are sending out. Having some visual reference is always better when you are approaching visual media.

If you do a book signing, bring a computer-generated, or professionally printed sign that tells attendees your immediately upcoming radio or TV dates.

If you do appearances in an area where you are also going to be doing a signing, give the host a legibly written note that tells him/her the name of the bookstore, the date, and the time, and ask him/her to make an announcement. That can usually be accommodated at the close of your segment.

If you make it onto the national TV talk shows make certain that the producer has a copy of the book to hold up. Get a 3/4-inch tape of the show to use as other opportunities present themselves (or for continuous showing in your memorial museum).

When you send out a press release, include a second sheet with abbreviations of all your best reviews, or positive abbreviations of your worst reviews. (You remember, the ones with all the ...'s in them.)

Publicity feeds on itself. Use whatever you can get to get whatever else you can.

17
One-Of-A-Kinds.

The last PR category on your list of what to do to make some noise on behalf of your book is *novelties*.

Novelties are one of a kind things like buttons or balloons that say "I Know From Crabs!" in large type and *"The Crabbers' Cookbook!"* in small type. Novelties are banners, key chains, pencils. They're playthings and geegaws. They could also be a one-time rental of the Fuji Blimp to flash your title across the sky. Or a direct mail pop-up clown. Or a real clown who serenades your praises at the International Book Fair. Novelties are anything that you can think of that won't get you arrested, that serves as a reminder of your book, and that you only have to do once or twice.

They are particularly good to offer bookstores as promotional attention-getters in the store when you are doing personal appearances, and to offer bookstore owners as premiums to get them to remember your title. These items cost something, so you have to decide if what they cost is worth their impact. You're not only figuring costs versus the return in royalties for *this* book, but for the next one.

Look in the Yellow Pages under *advertising specialties* if you want to hire the services of others to think up some cleverness on your behalf. Or check at your local stationery or office supply store. Local printers and quick-copy stores often offer printed novelty services. These places can usually tell you what color balloons they have in stock, and what they'll have to special order. They'll tell you what the charges are. This specialty category escalates expensively into renting three-story replica's of the Great Pumpkin, doing traffic-stopping billboards, sponsoring race cars—anything that puts your name and the name of your book in front of some group of potential buyers or influential people. If you have this kind of budget, consider hiring an ad or PR agency. It's faster, easier, and all you have to do is sign autographs. And checks.

If you don't have that kind of budget, and you own a computer, you don't have to spend that much. My computer's desktop publishing program created reminder postcards (Avery makes them for both tractor and laser printers) to send to radio program directors. My label maker program generated 2-1/2-inch, round self-adhesive stickers making nearly the entire American Booksellers' Convention instant **"Honorary Lesbians"** for about a penny apiece. And the last mailing my publisher did to bookstores had a printed day-glo paper airplane ready for fold up that came as a surprise bonus with a desktop publishing program.

The point about novelties is that they are meant to be one-of-a-kind freebies that make the recipient feel delighted to cross a room to get to or to open an envelope and find. They get people to feel good about you and your book and they get your title remembered. What should you do? Anything you can think of. And afford.

18
A Short Thought On A Computer.

Get one. Life and publicity opportunities are too short to try to do without.

Besides all the other things I have mentioned that my PC generated for my publicity campaigns, it's where I keep my Talk Radio database and keep track of all of the contacts by city, station, date, and book. The computer is, of course, where I wrote this—the least surprising of its uses.

The most creative of its uses is in helping you think up new things to do to generate publicity. Well, no, not all on its own. With a little help from a software program I strongly recommend to you. It's called **IdeaFisher** and its purpose and function is to serve as a fully implemented brainstorming tool. IdeaFisher is available in both Mac and PC formats for about a hundred bucks, and is like having six very bright friends with really creative memories sitting in your office with you whenever you need to generate an idea. You know, for all those times and places in this book where I said, "...or whatever's appropriate for *your* book."

Can you do it without a computer? Of course. You can do anything you set your mind to.

Should you do it without a computer?

Well, think how much more time you'd have to generate more publicity and maybe even write more books if you could let a machine do what you wouldn't have to do if you had one.

19
The Last Word.

Well, there you have it, the survey course in what you can do on your own, without a huge publicity mill or an oversized budget to get the word out on your book. That's what I know so far. It wasn't possible, in a book intended to be this brief, to cover everything. Still, I've tried to share the critical concepts, point you in the right directions, be specific enough to help you get some attention, and keep you from looking silly in the spotlight.

If you want to get publicity for your book, the principles are easy.

You have to 1) find the news value in what you wrote, or 2) find a way to make some attention-getting noise. Then you have to make that news or noise public property.

That's the gist. But, while the principles are easy, the real work of making that happen is hard. Or at least demanding. The amount of normal publicity you generate is pretty much in direct proportion to the amount of work you're willing to do to get it. By normal, I mean anything you can dream up on behalf of your book that won't land you on the cover of *People* magazine. Do something worthy of that kind of attention, and you won't need my advice on how to sell books. They'll roar off the shelves. (Although many of the things that might land you on the cover would also prevent you from enjoying any profit the book made while you were stamping out license plates.)

If you are interested in formally exploring the publicity possibilities for your book, go to your local public, college, or university library. They have volumes on this stuff. You can sign up at your community college for courses in public relations and advertising that can deliver far greater detail than this slim volume can.

But, honestly, to get yourself started all you really need to do is get started. Use the basic make news/make noise and baiting hooks principles in this book. Put your fertile imagination to work. What it takes, really, is a willingness to write your book's own destiny and a firm belief that you can.

The main thing about getting publicity though, is that the work is fun and so are the rewards. There is no question in my mind that you could work equally hard selling shoes or whole life insurance. Probably even work a lot harder. But at the end of that effort, when you emerge from cafes, strangers will not stop you to congratulate you.

So relax. And have some long-deserved fun making some news and some noise.

See you in the Green Room.

—Shelly Roberts

PARADIGM
Publishing Company

Paradigm Publishing Company, a woman owned press, was founded to publish works created within communities of diversity. These communities are empowering themselves and society by the creation of new paradigms which are inclusive of diversity. We are here to raise their voices.

To receive a free catalog, please write us as P.O. Box 3877, San Diego, CA 92163, or call (619) 234-7115, or fax us at (619) 234-2607.

Books Published by Paradigm Publishing:

Taken By Storm—Linda Kay Silva (Lesbian Mystery)

Expenses—Penny S. Lorio (Lesbian Romance)

Tory's Tuesday—Linda Kay Silva (Lesbian Romance)

Practicing Eternity—Carol Givens/L. Diane Fortier (Healing/Cancer)

Seasons of Erotic Love—Barbara Herrera (Lesbian Erotica)

Evidence of the Outer World—Janet Bohac (Women's Short Stories)

The Dyke Detector (How to Tell the Real Lesbians from Ordinary People)—Shelly Roberts/Ill.—Yani Batteau (Lesbian Humor)

Storm Shelter—Linda Kay Silva (Lesbian Mystery)

EMPATH—Michael Holloway (Gay Fiction/Sci-fi)

Hey Mom, Guess What! 150 Ways to Tell Your Mother
—Shelly Roberts/Ill.—Melissa Sweeney
(Lesbian/Gay Humor)

A Ship in the Harbor—Mary Heron Dyer (Lesbian Fiction)

Make News! Make Noise! How to Get Publicity for Your Book
—Shelly Roberts (How-To)

Golden Shores—Helynn Hoffa (Lesbian Romance/Mystery)

Weathering the Storm—Linda Kay Silva (Lesbian Mystery)